Lost Plantation

D1570354

JEFFERSON HISTORICAL SERIES VOLUME XVI

2005 Jefferson Parish Historical Commission
Jefferson Parish, Louisiana

Dr. Mary Grace Curry, Chairlady
Frank J. Borne Jr.
Bernice Grandison Dormio
Janet Sjoden Foster
Anne Escoffier Gauthreaux
Charmaine Currault Rini
Geraldine P. Vocke

www.JeffersonHistoricalSociety.com
Frank J. Borne Jr., Webmaster

Lost Plantation

THE RISE AND FALL OF SEVEN OAKS

MARC R. MATRANA

UNIVERSITY PRESS OF MISSISSIPPI / JACKSON

www.upress.state.ms.us

The University Press of Mississippi is a member of the
Association of American University Presses.

Copyright © 2005 by Marc R. Matrana
All rights reserved
Manufactured in the United States of America

Library of Congress Cataloging-in-Publication Data

Matrana, Marc R.
    Lost plantation : the rise and fall of Seven Oaks / Marc R. Matrana.— 1st ed.
      p. cm. — (Jefferson historical series ; v. 16)
    Includes bibliographical references and index.
    ISBN 1-57806-763-4 (alk. paper)
    1. Seven Oaks (La.) 2. Plantation life—Louisiana—Westwego—History—
19th century. 3. Zeringue, Camille. 4. Zeringue, Camille—Family. 5. Plantation
owners—Louisiana—Biography. 6. Slaveholders—Louisiana—Biography.
7. Businessmen—Louisiana—Biography. 8. Westwego (La.)—Biography.
9. Westwego (La.)—Social life and customs—19th century. I. Title. II. Series.

F379.S38M38 2005
307.72'09763'09034—dc22   2004028382

British Library Cataloging-in-Publication Data available

To my parents
Daniel A. and Jonnie Jordan Matrana

CONTENTS

ACKNOWLEDGMENTS

I extend my sincere appreciation to my dear friends Daniel P. Alario Sr. and Zenobia "Bebe" Rebstock Alario for their continuous support and assistance throughout this entire project and many others. Mr. Dan and Mrs. Bebe have been such an inspiration to me. I also thank Charmaine Currault Rini, a leader of many historical groups, who provided much encouragement and assistance by editing several late drafts of the manuscript. Dr. Mary Grace Curry edited a late draft of the manuscript and has been a constant support, and Betsy Swanson also provided much advice and direction, as did Frank J. Borne Jr. I am also indebted to Craig Gill, editor-in-chief at the University Press of Mississippi, for his support and belief in my work.

I also thank the Westwego Historical Society and all of its members; many of them provided encouragement and assistance. The late Sharon Favre spent countless hours translating documents for me; her time and very capable effort are so greatly appreciated. I thank Kermit Veneable for providing translation services as well. I would like to thank several people at Tulane University, including Dr. Chizuko Izawa, my mentor and friend. Dr. Beth Roberts read several early drafts of the manuscript and provided much insight and encouragement, as did Dr. John Dudley. Steven James of the Paul Tulane College also provided much assistance. I thank the Oscar Lee Putnum Cultural Endowment and its board, which provided generous financial support through its Cultural and Intellectual Enrichment Program.

I would like to thank the many people who shared their stories and memories of Seven Oaks, including Mildred Stehle Harris, former Jefferson Parish Councilman Lloyd Giardina, Elsie Favre, Dr. Henry and Kay Andressen, Andrea Taylor, Betty Grummer, and Dr. Bruce Pichoff, among many others. And I thank architect Davis Jahncke for sharing his collections and information about the plantation.

I must thank all of the teachers who encouraged my academic achievement through the years and who continue to support my endeavors: Hazel Rome, Tim and Lynn Stibrich, Carol Pearson, Lee Valance, and so many more. I must also thank several great journalism teachers who encouraged my love of writing: Jennifer Manuel, Della Domangue, Amy Bowmen, and, of course, my first journalism teacher, Daisy Orth. Mrs. Orth has been a beacon from day one and has never wavered in her support and in her friendship.

My many paternal aunts and uncles, my maternal grandmother, Wanda Jordan, and my godmother, Ann Sartin, have also been guiding lights. And, of course, the memory of my late paternal grandmother, Augustine Molaison Matrana, a descendent of the Zeringues, still inspires success. My extended family and friends have also provided much devotion and support through this project and many others.

Finally, and most important, I thank my parents, Daniel A. and Jonnie Jordan Matrana, for their unwavering love, support, and constant encouragement of all my varied endeavors. Without them none of this would have been possible. There are many, many others, too numerous to name, who provided assistance and helped me in so many ways, and to them I offer my sincere appreciation. Enjoy the book!

INTRODUCTION

What's in a name? That which we call a rose
By any other name would smell as sweet.

—WILLIAM SHAKESPEARE

The history of Louisiana's Seven Oaks Plantation is a regional tragedy of great significance, but it is also more. The story of Seven Oaks is an example of what can happen to any community when big business is allowed to trample history and heritage, and when local government forgets its ultimate responsibility to its own citizens.

Seven Oaks Plantation is a symbol—a symbol of the Old South. The once crumbling mansion and so many like it, from the Gulf to the East Coast, represent an era gone by, a time long ago faded into the past. These glorious structures also represent how we as a society deal with that troublesome, yet awesome, past.

The plantations of the South, and their inhabitants through the years, were not singular isolated entities in history but instead were tangled in a dense web of other plantations and plantation inhabitants like them all over the southern United States. This social, economic, and political web was embedded into the rich, intense culture of class and conflict, created and molded in a dynamic social hierarchy.

As the 1970s approached, Seven Oaks Plantation, one of these great symbols of the South's past, became the center of a major political battle. This struggle, which had been slowly coming to a boil, gained momentum and within a few short years exploded into an outright brawl over the fate of one of the nation's most historic properties.

Once the magnificent home of wealthy sugar planters, the Louisiana plantation in the middle of this fiasco stood crumbling as citizens, preservationists, and a few outspoken leaders begged for something to be done before this historic home was lost forever. Meanwhile, railroad officials who owned the historic property, along with many local politicians, rigidly fought any effort to save the crumbling mansion. What led to this fiery battle was a string of events as intriguing as the South itself. Indeed, these diverse events in the history of the plantation are what make the property so historic and win it the reverence of so many citizens. The plantation's unique history, from the earliest days of French colonization to contemporary times, is as varied as its ever-changing name.

The old plantation house, which once stood at the corner of River Road and the Old Spanish Trail (now Bridge City Avenue) in present-day Westwego, Louisiana, has been known by many names and has served many purposes. The French Minister of State and his noble associates first developed the area nearly concurrently with the founding of New Orleans. They called their early settlement Petit Desert. This primitive settlement, a swampy wilderness across the Mississippi River from the newly born Nouvelle Orleans, quickly developed into a busy depot for slaves and goods and later grew into a bustling plantation. As flags changed over Louisiana, so did the name of the plantation. By the time the Spanish had taken over, parts of the plantation were commonly known as Barataria.[1] At this time, much argument commenced over ownership. The plantation passed through several hands and finally ended up in the possession of the Zeringue family, who transformed the mediocre plantation into a thriving gem of sugar production. The Zeringues then lent their name to the plantation, calling it simply the Zeringue Plantation. Its success allowed planter Camille Zeringue the opportunity to build a large mansion on the plantation, replacing the smaller original house. The plantation's fortune and its flagship symbol, the columned master house, made it the envy of its neighbors along the Great River Road. As time passed, the plantation became somewhat of an icon, immortalized by famous writer and historian Grace King and others as Belle Dame (Beautiful Lady).[2] And then, years after the nation had been ravished by Civil War, Spaniard Pablo Sala, the founder of Salaville (the little settlement that would later grow into the City of Westwego), transformed the old plantation into an enchanting pleasure garden. He called his roadside resort Columbia Gardens, and, during the few short years of its operation, the attraction welcomed hundreds of thousands of visitors, both locals and tourists.

Local residents coined the unique name by which the old plantation at the corner of River Road and the Old Spanish Trail would become most well-known: Seven Oaks. The name, many say, refers to the seven large oak trees that originally surrounded the grand plantation mansion.[3] But others argue that this is not the case, pointing out that the significance of the number seven comes from the seven large columns on the sides of the house, as opposed to the customary eight.[4] Though we may never know whether the name Seven Oaks refers to trees or to columns, or, perhaps, even both, we do know that the plantation was an important monument to the South's heritage—a symbol of the past and all its facets.

The plantation saw the history of Louisiana and the South unfold through the years from the earliest colonial settlements to contemporary times. By examining the history of Seven Oaks, we examine the history of America. We can easily see how events of the day affected the plantation and the lives of those who lived and worked there on an intimate level. We can also see how the plantation and those like it affected the events of the past.

Petit Desert . . . Barataria . . . Zeringue Plantation . . . Belle Dame . . . Columbia Gardens . . . Seven Oaks . . . regardless of its name, the great plantation, which once thrived near the edge of present-day Westwego, Louisiana, is now lost, never to return. All that remains are the fading memories of those whose lives were touched by this Belle Dame among plantations. Today, on the site of the plantation's columned mansion, large, rusty petroleum storage tanks dot the area where the formal gardens of this unique home once welcomed distinguished guests. A few obscure images, as well as a handful of old sources, weave a rich tale of how this great plantation rose from the muddy banks of the Mississippi River to become one of the earliest and most extraordinary of its kind in Louisiana. These accounts and sources tell of the people who lived at Seven Oaks, who died at Seven Oaks, and whose lives were forever intertwined with this majestic plantation. They tell of the plantation's last breaths amid a great political battle between those who wished to restore and preserve the plantation's great house and its memory and those who would rather see it go. Most important, these sources tell how our nation and our people were robbed of a wonderful historical treasure.

By analyzing the events leading to the destruction of Seven Oaks, we may gain a greater understanding of the political and social intricacies involved in the failed preservation efforts. With knowledge of how the preservation of this structure, one of the South's largest and most historic plantation mansions, failed, we may be able to approach future preservation efforts with greater awareness of the multifaceted details that both facilitate and encumber the preservation of America's built environments.

Lost Plantation

CHAPTER ONE

Petit Desert

In the name of the Almighty, all powerful, invincible and victorious
Prince Louis, the Great, by the grace of God, King of France and of
Navarre, fourteenth of this name this day 9th April, 1682, I by virtue
of the commission of His Majesty which I hold in hand have taken and
do take possession, in the name of His Majesty and of the successors of
his crown, of this country of Louisiana.

—RENE ROBERT CAVELIER, SIEUR DE LA SALLE

It has been said that "the history of Louisiana flows from the Mississippi
River," and, even from the earliest times, this seems to hold true.[1] The
Mississippi was a pinnacle of native civilization, and it was the focal point
of early European exploration of the area. It was along this mighty river
that in 1682 explorer Rene Robert Cavelier, sieur de La Salle, traveled to
survey and explore the region. In April of that year, La Salle claimed the
land through which the river flowed, from the Appalachians to the Rockies,
in the name of Louis XIV, King of France. He named the land Louisiana in
honor of the king and his bride, Queen Anne. Five years later, La Salle
attempted to establish a colony in Louisiana, but his efforts led to his early
death. In 1698, Pierre Le Moyne, sieur d'Iberville, successfully established a
permanent French colony in Louisiana when he built a fort at Biloxi in
present-day Mississippi. One year later, Iberville's brother, Jean Baptiste Le
Moyne, sieur de Bienville, traveled the Mississippi River, where he found
an important location for a settlement.

The primary goal of Louisiana settlements was to prevent England from
gaining control over the mouth of the Mississippi River. With their
colonies in present-day Canada and Louisiana, the French sought to limit
the British colonies on the eastern seaboard.[2] Bienville became governor

of Louisiana, and, in 1718, he established a settlement at the location that he had visited on the Mississippi River several years earlier. He called the settlement Nouvelle Orléans, in honor of the duc d'Orléans.

Across the Mississippi River from the primitive settlement of Nouvelle Orléans, a few leagues upriver lay a vast wilderness territory that would soon welcome its first permanent settlers. Long before this land was home to Seven Oaks Plantation, this undeveloped tract was known to the earliest French settlers as Petit Desert (Little Desert or Little Wilderness). Although the French word "desert" may bring to mind sand dunes and cacti for English speakers, it translates to more of an undeveloped wilderness rather than a true desert. It was actually swamp land, thick and muddy. As with most of southern Louisiana, water surrounded the land: a curve of the Mississippi River wrapped itself around the majority of the settlement, and wetlands, lakes, and bayous lurked nearby.

John Law's Company of the Indies, which then controlled Louisiana, granted Petit Desert to the French minister of state, Monseigneur LeBlanc, on November 18, 1719, as a concession one year after the French established their settlement at Nouvelle Orléans. LeBlanc shared this concession with three of his associates: the Marquis d'Asfeld, marshal of France and director general of fortifications; the Compte de Belle Isle, lieutenant-general of the King's Armies; and Gerard Michel de la Jonchere, treasurer general of the Military Order of St. Louis. These distinguished French gentlemen raised among themselves a sum of 400,000 livres[3] for this establishment, which also included two other land grants, one below New Orleans on the west bank of the river known as Chaouachas[4] and a second at Natchez. Because the land was nestled along the bank of the Mississippi River, LeBlanc's associates used Petit Desert as a depot for slaves and goods, which they transported to and from the other concessions of the French minister of state. As a result, settlers developed Petit Desert earlier than the other two concessions. The settlements also later became the port from which goods and crops produced in the French colony were exported for sale.[5] (See fig. 1.)

The first people who settled the swampy Petit Desert area, later destined to become a bustling plantation, set sail from the Port of L'Orient in France on June 30, 1720.[6] Troops, controlled by French Minister of State LeBlanc's associates, accompanied Captain Igance Francois Broutin on his voyage.

In his article for the Historic American Building Survey (HABS), noted Louisiana architectural historian Samuel Wilson Jr.[7] suggested that the Marquis d'Asfeld may have handpicked Broutin for the position of captain because of his prior military service with the engineer corps in France. After arriving at Petit Desert, Broutin cleared the land for the establishment of a trading post.[8] Later, Broutin became the engineer-in-chief of Louisiana and the architect of the Ursuline Convent[9] (which existed from 1734 to 1752 and preceded the still standing "old convent" that today is the oldest building in the Mississippi Valley), as well as the majority of official buildings within the French colony of Louisiana.[10] Interestingly, there was a connection between Broutin, who designed the Ursuline Convent, and Michael Zehringer, the progenitor of all "Zeringue" families in Louisiana, who built the first Ursuline Convent. These two men, both of whom had a hand in building New Orleans, also had an indirect connection to the great plantation. Broutin carried the first settlers from France to Petit Desert, whereas many years later, Michael Zehringer's descendants transformed the Petit Desert settlement into one of the greatest plantations in Louisiana.

Soon after Broutin and his settlers arrived in Louisiana, Governor Vaudreuil[11] received a letter stating that Broutin "was then (1720–1721) employed in the said concessions [and] improved and cleared the one called Little Desert, which is the first establishment made in this colony by the said Marshals de Belle Isle and d'Asfeld."[12]

Petit Desert continued to flourish and was quickly developed as it served as a trading post depot for slaves and goods transported to and from the other concessions of the French minister of state. Little is known of the European settlers who inhabited the area, but their lives, like those of their counterparts in New Orleans, were filled with hardships and labor. These settlers cleared some of the land and probably grew a variety of crops at Petit Desert for both sale and their own consumption. This early development and the production of a built environment on the property created a foundation for the larger agricultural, architectural, and other developments that were to come.

The settlers continued to improve the land by building a variety of structures and shelters. Early structures in colonial Louisiana were crude by contemporary European standards, usually being constructed of whatever indigenous materials could be obtained. Rudimentary structural frameworks

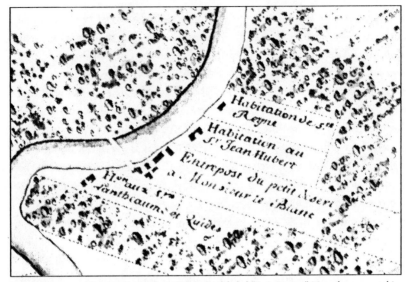

Fig. 1. A 1723 map showing the LeBlanc Concession labeled "Petit Desert." Note that even at this early date the plantation had a relatively extensive built environment. Also note the estate had neighbors on both sides. Photo courtesy of the Edward E. Ayer Collection, The Newberry Library, Chicago.

were filled with mud and moss to make adobe-type walls and a thatched roof or one of bark was added on top.[13]

A 1723 map of the area clearly shows at least six buildings on the property, many more than any neighboring settlements. Although the buildings are certainly not drawn to scale, their general arrangement may have been fairly accurate. The structures seem to have been aligned haphazardly, with most lining the riverfront. Included in this set of buildings was one particularly large central building that may have served any number of functions, including a residence. (See fig. 1.)

Whereas the European settlers at Petit Desert were probably the more permanent residents of the area, they were certainly not the only ones. Petit Desert grew because of its use as a depot and a trading post. Of the commodities shipped to and from this economic hub, the most anticipated were enslaved human beings, whose labor the colonists desperately sought. Most of these slaves were of African descent; however, others, including Native Americans, were often enslaved during this time period. Of those slaves transported from Africa, many had been kidnapped by trans-Atlantic slave traders. Others may have been sold to the traders by fellow Africans from rival tribes or, rarely, by their own kinsmen. These people were ripped away from everything they knew and packed into ships that transported them to the primitive French settlements of Louisiana. They crossed the middle passage in chains, arrived in an unfamiliar land, and were forced to toil for the rest of their days. About two-thirds of the Africans brought to the colony by French slave traders were from Senegambia, a geographic and cultural region between the Senegal and Gambia rivers. Others brought to Louisiana were Malinke-speaking Bambaras from the western interior of Africa. About half of these slaves, like Native Americans, succumbed to a variety of European diseases for which they had no resistance.[14]

The enslaved Africans arriving at the French minister of state's depot at Petit Desert likely experienced atrocious conditions on their journey halfway around the world from their homeland. Inconceivable terror, sorrow, and anger must have besieged them as they were unloaded into the strange settlement; a place they never knew existed but now saw with their own eyes.

Historians have long had a tendency to view newly enslaved Africans, such as those arriving at Petit Desert, as a somewhat homologous group; this, however, could not be further from the truth. Slaves on any given slave ship were likely to have come from a number of various tribes or communities. Members of such tribes shared a unique history, culture, and often a separate language, quite distinct from that of their neighboring communities. For the most part, Africans were as diverse, if not more so, as the peoples of the European continent. Sometimes these groups had long histories of interaction on the mother continent—with both positive and negative consequences. But, despite their varied pasts, the newly arriving slave populace quickly found shared meaning through the horrors of their condition as human chattel.

As slaves continued to arrive at Petit Desert and other established settlements in the colony, the population of the area grew. In a census taken in 1721, New Orleans had a total population of 470 people—277 whites, 172 black slaves, and 21 Native American slaves. One year later, New Orleans became the capital of the colony, as power was transferred from Biloxi. Nine years later, in 1731, Louisiana officially became a French Crown Colony with a population that had expanded to nearly 8,000, including enslaved persons.

With this growing population and increased economic potential, the original owners of the Petit Desert land grant decided to redeem the cash value of their estate. French Minister of State LeBlanc and his associates sold their settlement on January 28, 1738, to Joseph Assailly and Charles Favre Daunoy. Records described the property at that time as "fourteen arpents of land frontage by the ordinary depth, situated at the place called the 'Little Desert', about one league above New Orleans on the other side of the river, with the huts, appurtenances and dependencies thereon."[15] Together the two men further improved the LeBlanc settlement, expanding agricultural operations. Although no records exist that definitively state which crops Assailly and Daunoy grew at Petit Desert, they probably raised rice, the most successful crop in early French Louisiana. Rice had been introduced as a major crop in 1719, when two slave ships brought barrels of seed along with slaves experienced in growing the crop.[16] They may also have raised tobacco or indigo, which were relatively successful cash crops. They may have raised corn, squash, and potatoes, indigenous crops that Native Americans taught the French how to grow.[17] Other staples were cultivated in lesser quantities, but, to the French settlers' disappointment, wheat was not a successful crop in the colony. Neither sugar nor cotton was a major crop at this time, as the process for converting cane juice to storable sugar granules was not known to the colonists, and the machine that could separate seed from short-fiber American cotton had not yet been invented. Assailly and Daunoy probably raised livestock and poultry on their plantation, and throughout this time, citrus, peaches, figs, and plums were all popular fruits raised in Louisiana. During this period, for the first time in its short history, Louisiana was self-sufficient in meeting its demand for food, with the exception of wine and wheat, which still had to be imported. The agricultural methods used by Assailly and Daunoy were similar to those of others of their time and included the most basic farming techniques. Farming conditions in Louisiana bore little resemblance to those in the mother country, which left settlers to endure a great deal of trial-and-error before agriculture could flourish.[18]

On March 6, 1752, Daunoy acquired Assailly's interest in the plantation by a transaction at Cap Francois. After that, Daunoy lived only a short time, and his plantation was passed to his widow.[19] Claude Joseph Villars Dubreuil Jr., son of the contractor for the King's buildings and works in

Louisiana, acquired the plantation from the Widow Daunoy in 1759. There is some indication that the plantation was temporarily stagnant and possibly abandoned after Daunoy's death. Dubreuil may have occupied the abandoned estate before actually purchasing it. At this time, part of the land was known as Barataria and was then described as "containing sixteen arpents of frontage by the ordinary depth of forty arpents situated on the other side of the Mississippi River at about a league from this town."[20] Dubreuil is noted to have complained that wild horses from the herd of Jean Baptiste Massey, established along Bayou des Familles, were wreaking havoc on his property.[21]

At some time, a canal was dug on the property that connected the river to Bayou Segnette, allowing further access to the properties and land behind the plantation. It is quite possible that the canal was dug by Dubreuil, as he may have been inspired by his father, who earlier had successfully built a canal at present-day Harvey connecting the river to Bayou Barataria. The canal at Petit Desert served the plantation's transportation needs, including transporting logs from the back swamps. It was also extremely important for transporting shells. Dubreuil owned property in the Barataria region that contained giant shell middens, enormous mounds of shells that had been piled over decades by the Native Americas as they ate indigenous shellfish. These shells were often brought from the backlands to the river to be used in making lime for building materials and in the construction of roads, at great profit. The canal, however, would be considered small by today's standards. These canals were of great service to the French King, as they transported boats, filled with Navy troops, to the war against the Chickasaws.[22]

By the 1760s, Petit Desert had grown from a backwater trading post and depot to a fine plantation, but soon the lives of the plantation's inhabitants would be forever altered as flags changed over the area. The French made a secret agreement with Spain, ceding all the Louisiana Territory west of the Mississippi River (including Petit Desert) and the "Isle of Orleans" (New Orleans) on the east bank of the river. By the 1762 Treaty of Fontainebleau, Spain gained control of this land. All of Louisiana east of the Mississippi River, except New Orleans, fell under control of the British by the 1763 Treaty of Paris. The predominantly French residents of New Orleans, accustomed to French rule, rebelled against the Spanish, but the rebellion was sternly suppressed, and Spanish domination was confirmed. Life in a Spanish colony was much different for the residents of Petit Desert, but the colonists persevered through the establishment of Spanish rule and soon flourished.

In the late 1760s, an interesting situation arose between the plantation's owner and Spanish officials. Dubreuil appears to have fallen into much debt. Spanish judicial records contain several lively accounts of the lawsuits against Dubreuil and the various events and actions resulting from them. Samuel Wilson Jr. notes that by February 1768, "Joseph Maison, sheriff [was] ordered to seize property of Villars [Dubreuil] in execution of judgments of the Council in favor of Mr. Gerardo de Villemond for what was due Mr. Dauberville's heirs."[23] Spanish judicial records suggest that the seizure was prevented by Dubreuil although other historical sources recount that the seizure did occur (perhaps after the creation of the Spanish records).

Regardless of whether the seizure did actually result or not, the worst of Dubreuil's problems were still to come. Suits were brought against him by his creditors, including his two sons-in-law (representing Dubreuil's own daughters), Marie Francoise Petit de Coulange (the widow of Colonel Pedro de Villemont), and Francisco Bouligny for his wife, Maria Luisa Dauberville. Spanish Governor Unzaga commissioned Cecilio Odoardo to make a complete inventory of all property belonging to Dubreuil.[24] Spanish records recount that Odoardo made his way to the plantation accompanied by several others, including the "escribano" (a general secretary of accounts or records). Spanish judicial records recount what took place: "When they arrived they saw a woman in one of the doors of the house together with Juan [Jean Louis] Trudeau, son-in-law of Villars [Dubreuil]. When she saw the ministers of the court coming the woman went into the house and closed the doors and Trudeau remained on the gallery and accosted the commissioner, Odoardo." Dubreuil approached from another house on the property, which he stated was his home. He refused to let the officers make an inventory of his possessions and denied owing anything to Coulange or Bouligny. He asked to see an official order from the governor, but even when one was produced, Dubreuil still refused to allow the inventory to be taken. For the indiscretion of closing the doors on officials and the refusal of allowing a proper inventory to be taken, Dubreuil was taken into custody and jailed in the military prison of the providence.[25]

While in prison, Dubreuil received an official visit from Governor Unzaga, who proceeded to interrogate him. Unzaga was accompanied by the assessor general, an interpreter named Jacinto Panis, and the escribano, Andres Almonestar. Dubreuil told the governor that he had not allowed the officers of the court to make an inventory of his property because he did not recognize them. He further elaborated that he had only been to the city a few times, and, during his visits there, he had no interaction with these officials and, therefore, was unable to recognize them when they called upon him at his plantation. Dubreuil stated that if he had sinned against the courts it was by ignorance, not by volition. When asked why the doors of his home were shut against the ministers of the court, he told Unzaga that his daughter had closed the doors of the house because the sun was shining in one of the rooms where clothes were being ironed. He also explained that this was not his home, as he lived in another residence on the property. Unzaga finally questioned Dubreuil about a letter he had written on the day the officials visited his plantation. The letter, according to the Spanish records, contained a variety of insults against the officers and ridiculed them mercilessly. Dubreuil had no excuse for this except to plead with the governor and assure him that he meant no harm or ridicule by his letter.

Despite Dubreuil's many attempts to not pay his creditors, including two of his own daughters, the Court of Governor Unzaga ruled against him. His property was seized and auctioned on behalf of his creditors. Interestingly, the same creditors obtained most of the auctioned property.

The intricacies of the case of Dubreuil not only reveal the richness and depth of the beginnings of the great plantation commonly known today as Seven Oaks but also allow a glimpse of the cultural and political atmosphere of Louisiana during this turbulent time. While Spanish judicial records written from a Spanish point of view may well color the details of the case in a way that marginalizes Dubreuil's side of the story, they also illuminate broader issues of the day. For example, the case illustrates the complexities that resulted from the Spanish rule of a predominantly French population. Although Dubreuil's debts were certainly genuine (genuine enough for his daughters to file suit against him), the establishment of Spanish rule over French culture probably added to the intricacies of this case. Spanish judicial proceedings were somewhat different from those of the previous French rulers, and it is obvious that this change caused Dubreuil many problems. This is not to suggest that Dubreuil did not indeed seek to abandon the responsibilities associated with paying his creditors but simply to note that Dubreuil may well have been intimidated by strange officials from an unfamiliar country, speaking a foreign language. He was obviously unaccustomed to Spanish judicial proceedings and understood little about the manner in which the governor and his courts handled this affair. This was not a rare, isolated event but echoes what was happening in the wider colony. Despite the economic growth spearheaded during Spanish rule, French colonists never really accepted their Spanish leaders.

In the early 1770s, Pierre Delisle (Delille or Felila) Dupart purchased a portion of Petit Desert from the auction of the seized property of Dubreuil. In March 1775, Dupart sold his interest in the plantation to Jean-Louis Trudeau, son-in-law of former owner, Dubreuil. The act of sale stated, "I, Don Pedro Delile called Dupare (sic) . . . sell really and in fact to Don [Jean] Louis Trudeau who was Alcalde of this city, a plantation named Little Desert with about twenty arpents of front on the river, and a depth of forty or more, some two leagues distant from the city, situated on the other side of the river, bordered on one side by the land . . . and on the other by that of Louis Harang . . . that belongs to me by having bought it at the auction, sale of the goods of Don Claudio Joseph Villars." Samuel Wilson Jr. notes in his 1953 Historic American Buildings Survey that Trudeau was probably the father or brother of the famous Spanish surveyor Don Carlos Laveau Trudeau. At this time, the plantation's neighbors were Jean Baptiste Senet and Louis Harang.[26]

Jean Louis Trudeau owned the plantation until 1785, when he sold twelve arpents to his neighbor Alexandre Harang.[27] Harang continued to operate the plantation and profit from its agricultural development and continued to improve the built environment, setting the groundwork for the much larger operations that were to come.

Harang owned much land up and down the river and, like Dubreuil, also owned property in the back swamp region. He acquired land at Grand Coquille and certainly used the canal for transporting shells from the middens there to sell. Also, logging was probably similarly done in the backlands, and the canal would have been a great transportation utility in this enterprise. Furthermore, game, goods, and perhaps even slaves may have been regularly traded via this important communication channel. During this period, the Spanish instituted harsh laws regarding trading, and such a waterway may have been used by French settlers for a multitude of illegal commerce.[28]

Records indicate that during the time he owned the plantation, Harang was actively involved in the purchase and sale of numerous enslaved persons. For example, in April 1793, he sold a twenty-five-year-old black man named Juan Luis for six hundred pesos to Santiago Roman of Opelousas, Louisiana. The slave was then sent to St. Landry Parish. Harang also often purchased slaves during the time he owned the plantation. In 1792, he bought a male slave, also twenty-five years of age, from Paul Toups. This enslaved man, called Pierot, was born in Bamana and spoke one of the Mande languages.[29] Clearly Harang played an active economic role in his community, and one can assume that he was trying to build an ideal labor force while maximizing his profits.

Nine years after purchasing the plantation in 1794, Harang sold part of his land interests to his son-in-law, Michel Zeringue. The land was sold, the act of sale stated, "with all the buildings which are constructed on it, their implements, utensils, groves and fences . . . with the expressed condition that Monsieur Lebreton shall enjoy the canal which passes by said land while he is a neighbor."[30] Certainly, by this time the above-mentioned canal was still a great utility to the plantation's owners. Zeringue owned property at Grand Temple[31] on the western end of Lake Salvador, which was known for its abundant shell middens, the largest in the Barataria estuary. And like those who came before him, Zeringue used the plantation's canal to bring the riches of the back swamp to the river for his profit. The canal remained, by today's standards, little more than a large ditch, but, nonetheless, it served crucial functions for the plantation. The canal was often used by slaves who were instructed to paddle through the nearby bayous and swamps to gather wood and moss for use on the plantation. It also provided a means of communication between plantations and a sort of privileged commerce for those allowed to navigate between its narrow banks. Although just a ditch, the little canal at Petit Desert accomplished crucial tasks, and it preceded a much larger, more ambitious waterway that was to come. This smaller canal and its surrounding infrastructure provided a great foundation upon which further developments and improvements would later commence.[32]

The Zeringues and Their Plantation

The cession of Louisiana and the Floridas by Spain to France works most sorely on the United States.

—THOMAS JEFFERSON, 1802

Michel Zeringue, grandson of the well-known colonial builder, Michael Zehringer, purchased the Little Desert plantation from his father-in-law, Alexandre Harang, in 1794. The purchase included all the buildings and improvements on the plantation and the canal that had been dug there. Zeringue continued to improve and expand the plantation and farm its lands, cultivating a foundation upon which his son would develop an even greater estate.

Zeringue's tenure as plantation owner was not without controversy. The parish court records and New Orleans City Court records are filled with suits filed against and filed by Zeringue. A number of these legal pleadings involved Alexandre Daspit St. Amant, who was apparently a close business associate of Zeringue. In one such suit, Zeringue sued St. Amant for $2,326.66. The suit states the defendant was at one time indebted to Zeringue for the sum of $8,000, plus 8 percent interest annually, which was to be paid in full within two or three years. Apparently, St. Amant failed to pay the remainder of this debt, and the court ruled in Zeringue's favor.

Another similar and interesting suit was filed against John McDonogh,[1] a successful merchant who is best known for his exceptional generosity to the local school system. In this preceding, Zeringue sought $189.50, plus interest and costs from McDonogh. Evidently, Zeringue's slaves had made some repairs on the levee at the McDonogh plantation, and McDonogh subsequently refused to reimburse him for this work. The built levees, which provided protection from the flood waters of the Mississippi, were a vital part of the physical plantation infrastructure. It was the responsibility of each planter to maintain the levee along his property, and continuous repairs were necessary. Such strife between planters over their levees was not uncommon, as a weak area in one planter's levee system could possibly lead to a crevasse and ultimately flood many plantations in the area.

Throughout his ownership of the plantation, Zeringue transferred various parts of it to members of his family. Portions of the property would continue to change hands throughout most of the life of the plantation. Zeringue's brother, Jean Louis, owned three arpents of land bordering that of his brother. Jean Louis lived there with his wife, Anna Constance Constant, in a two-story, eight-room house that measured thirty-two by fifty feet.[2] Their property "contained a corn house, a kitchen, four slave cabins, an old rice mill, and a small crop of corn and rice." The couple raised two daughters there: Constance, who was baptized on May 8, 1800, and Marie Elisa, who was born about 1806.[3]

Now under Spanish rule, the once ailing French colony of Louisiana gained an economic vitality that it had never known before. During this time, agriculture began to flourish in and around New Orleans, and the area grew into a major port. All this prosperity and trade meant success for planters, including Zeringue.

Five years after the Zeringue family purchased its plantation, Spain declared war on Great Britain, an act that changed the face of Louisiana forever and ultimately had a great impact on the history of the Zeringue family and its plantation. Louisiana's governor, Bernardo de Gálvez, became active in the war by capturing the cities of Baton Rouge, Natchez, Mobile, and Pensacola from Great Britain. In 1800, French Emperor Napoleon forced the retrocession of Louisiana to France. King Charles IV of Spain reluctantly gave in to the French emperor, and, in the secret Treaty of San Ildefonso, Spain returned control of Louisiana to France. Once word of the treaty reached Washington, D.C., it caused great concerns for the United States, which relied on the major port at New Orleans and the transportation route through the Mississippi River.

At this time, President Thomas Jefferson attempted to purchase "the Isle of Orleans" from France, but, to the surprise of many, including the president himself, Napoleon agreed to sell all of Louisiana to the United States. The United States paid less than three cents an acre for more than 828,000 square miles of land. This, the greatest real estate transaction in history, came to be known as the Louisiana Purchase. It doubled the size of the still young United States and paved the way for future westward expansion.

The Zeringues had witnessed their home being transferred among three different nations and were themselves under the rule of those three countries (Spain, France, and the United States) in a period of only a few years. When Zeringue purchased the plantation from his father-in-law in 1794, the land was under Spanish rule, where it remained until 1800, when Louisiana was transferred to the French. Only three years later, Louisiana became the territory of the United States. All the while, life on the plantation went on, and day-to-day business was initially unchanged.

In 1812, the Territory of Orleans was admitted to the Union as the State of Louisiana. Initially, little changed in Louisiana as it entered statehood; both French and Spanish influences were still very prevalent throughout the area, and agriculture continued to flourish during this, the golden age of plantation life in Louisiana. Statehood, however, quickly brought great opportunities to planters. Michel Zeringue and his family continued to prosper and eagerly shared in the success that statehood afforded.

Michel Zeringue and his wife, Marie Josephine Harang (also known as Josette), had at least six children: Michel Jr., Camille, Marie Aime Azelie, Adele, Edmond, and Marianna Arelie.[4] Michel Zeringue died sometime after 1810, leaving his wife and children to care for his large plantation.[5]

Records indicate that Michel's widow took over the operation of the plantation to provide for her children. It is also clear that at some point her son Camille became a partner with his widowed mother. At this time in Louisiana, a widow held quite a unique position in society. Married women were tied to their husbands and were expected to "honor and obey" them in every way. In the patriarchal culture of the South, a married woman relied on her husband for her every necessity; he was indeed the center of her universe, and as such he was also her master. With her husband gone, the Widow Zeringue had greater freedoms and unique prestige within the community.[6]

Unlike other women of her time, the widowed plantation mistress was free to own property and to participate fully in the economics of her day, controlling her property and running the plantation. Widows also were free to travel, receive guests, and visit friends without having to seek a husband's approval or permission.[7] Evidence suggests that this is exactly what the Widow Zeringue did. She ran the plantation and did so quite successfully. Emancipation records from 1846 show that the Widow Zeringue emancipated two of her female slaves, Saraphine and Celeste, and their children.[8] She did so without the aid or objection of a husband.

This is not to say that the plight of the plantation matriarch was without hardships. It was not uncommon for the problems of grieving plantation widows to be compounded by financial concerns, as even many of the wealthiest planters kept their finances in much disarray. And, although widows like Zeringue did have more freedom than their non-widowed counterparts, they were still women in a society dominated by men. A widow, no matter how prestigious or wealthy, was not the social or political equal of a white man.[9]

The one advantage that the Widow Zeringue had over many widows of her day was that she had a strong-minded young son, Camille, who at some point aided her in running the plantation. Evidence exists to suggest that he may have entered into partnership with his mother gradually, first by aiding her in the day-to-day operations of the plantation, and then later taking over much of the work on behalf of his mother and siblings. What is clear is that even as late as the 1850s, the Widow Zeringue played a major economic and administrative role in the life of the plantation. In P. A. Champomier's 1849–50 "Statement of The Sugar Crop Made in Louisiana," she is still mentioned along with her son as having produced two hundred hogshead of sugar, with loss to overflow. But, even as the Widow Zeringue held on to her position as matriarch of the family and the plantation, it was Camille who took over the role of planter.

Planters like Camille Zeringue made up a unique aristocracy, which played a central role in politics, economic life, and society in the southern states. Zeringue was among the preeminent of this elite group, and, by any definition, he was certainly an aristocrat. He and his family commanded immense wealth and enjoyed its ensuing power. This position gave him the credentials to participate in the important social, political, and economic circles of the area.

In December 1828, Zeringue became involved in a lawsuit that would demand his attention for years to come. The suit sprang from a business deal in which he sold a steam engine to Joseph Dyer Parsons, who was representing his interest in the Holmes and Parsons Iron Foundry.

The very fact that Zeringue owned a steam engine tells much about his plantation operations, as well as the generalized progress and industrialization that was taking place in Louisiana agricultural operations at the time. Though a few planters rejected new technology that was emerging during the decades prior to the Civil War in favor of more time-honored techniques, many embraced such progress. Obviously, Zeringue was one of the plantation owners who held little apprehension at the idea of such advancements.

While many have assumed that industrial progress and the institution of slavery were incompatible, this notion has recently been brought into question. Progress and often swift industrialization in Louisiana's cane fields coexisted and were even spurred by the institution of slavery. Zeringue and most of his fellow planters, rather than rejecting capitalistic progress, embraced industrialization both prior to and after the emancipation of their slave labor force.[10]

Zeringue's ultimate motivation for selling this questioned steam engine is difficult to speculate; however, because he asked the then large sum of four hundred dollars for it, it is unlikely that is was for scrap iron. Perhaps Zeringue was replacing the engine with a newer or more improved model.

It is clear, however, that Zeringue did not receive the money he was owed for this piece of property and therefore found it necessary to file suit against Joseph Parsons and Eleazor Holmes. Zeringue's neighbor along the river, fellow planter and attorney Charles Derbigny,[11] represented him in this matter. The suit was originally filed on December 16, 1828, and subsequently resulted in the arrest of both Holmes and Parsons, who immediately posted bonds ensuring they would not flee the state. The original petition stated:

> The petition of Camille Zeringue Planter . . . that he sold and delivered to Holmes and Parson trading under the term of Holmes and Parsons and residing in the City of New Orleans, a steam engine for the sum of four hundred dollars which they had promised to pay cash.
>
> And your petitioners further show that although they have since been frequently amicably requested to pay the said sum yet they have always negated and refused to do it. Wherefore your petitioner [asks] that in consideration of the said Holmes and the said Parson to be arrested and compelled each to

furnish sufficient security that they will not leave that state and that they may be cited to answer this petition and that they may be condemned . . . to pay the said sum of four hundred dollars with interest and costs.

C. Derbigny
Atty. For Plaintiff

Parsons's attorney, A. Mace, answered the suit with a written response indicating that his client had sold all his interest in the Holmes and Parsons Iron Foundry to Edward E. Parker. Attached to this document was a handwritten copy of the record of this transaction. The text stated that Parsons had indeed sold his interest along with any incurred debts to Edward Parker for the sum of one thousand dollars and two slaves, one twenty-one-year-old man called Anderson and a second slave of the same name whose age was not stated.

Edward Parker's attorney subsequently responded that his client was not responsible for this debt as it had not been specifically mentioned to him at the time of the sale. Parsons, of course, disagreed.

Witness testimony by Holmes and others indicated that Zeringue did strike a bargain with Parsons for the sale of this steam engine on behalf of the iron foundry. The agreed-upon price was indeed four hundred dollars. Parsons visited the Zeringue Plantation in person and transported the steam engine along with some broken castings in a hull boat along the river. Witnesses are said to have seen the engine's arrival at the iron foundry.

The case raged on for years in the court, but despite bickering between the parties at every turn, a final judgment was entered on behalf of the plaintiff. Holmes and Parsons were each ordered to pay $200 plus interest at a rate of 5 percent annually from the date the original suit was filed, to Zeringue, along with court costs of $63.56. The court sided with Parker, and his argument that he was not explicitly informed of this particular debt upon his purchase of the iron foundry was apparently enough of an explanation to release him from any responsibility.

This case, while interesting in its own right, provides insight into the world of Zeringue and the society that he dominated. He was a steadfast and unyielding man, content to forge ahead for years in order to see that justice and his interests were served. He was unwavering in his adamant beliefs, and his uncompromising desire for that which was owed to him is obvious.

The court's ultimate sympathy toward the plight of Camille Zeringue, which eventually led to a decision in his favor, while probably legitimate and warranted, was also surely colored by his station in life. The planter elite to which Zeringue belonged was to Louisiana and the South as a whole a class like no other. Planters commanded, if not demanded, respect and privilege from the society that they had come to dominate. The courts may have been influenced by Zeringue's status as a planter, a title that during Louisiana's so-called Golden Age brought with it societal advantages and benefits like no other.

One of the benefits afforded to the planter elite was the freedom to participate in politics. While lower-class white male citizens often shared the legal right to participate in such discourse, societal and economic norms of the day ensured that much political power was reserved for plantation owners and others of their general social class. Zeringue took part in politics with great enthusiasm, and, along with his fellow planters in neighboring areas, he created a local government to serve the needs of the community.

Zeringue and his contemporaries were tired of the inconvenience of living under the rule of the Orleans Parish government. In order to conduct official business, it was necessary for them to travel to New Orleans—not an easy task considering there were no bridges over the Mississippi River or automobiles to traverse the miles. In order to remedy the situation, Zeringue and other prominent men of the area sought to create a new parish to serve their areas, making it easier for them to travel to the parish seat. In 1825, plantation owners, including Zeringue, and other businessmen living outside New Orleans petitioned for the creation of Jefferson Parish from a portion of Orleans Parish. With this move, the men sought to control their developments and ultimately to dominate their own economic and political interests even more. The Louisiana Legislature officially granted the gentlemen's requests for a new parish, establishing it on February 11, 1825, during the administration of Governor Henry Johnson. Originally to be named Tchoupitoulas, the new parish ultimately took the name Jefferson, in honor of President Thomas Jefferson, under whose administration the Louisiana Purchase was made. The seat of government was originally established at Lafayette in present-day New Orleans but was later moved to Carrollton also in present-day New Orleans.[12]

An 1834 Act of the Louisiana Legislature firmly organized the police jury system, creating more standardized systems of parish government throughout the state. Jefferson Parish, along with the other parishes of the state, adopted the organizational structure of government outlined in this act. The act set forth that the parish police jury itself was to be a body of no less than eight and no more than twelve elected members. The act called for the division of a parish into wards equal in number to the number of police jurors. The jurors were to meet and elect a president, who would sign contracts and preside at meetings, and a secretary-treasurer, who was responsible for recording the proceedings of each session. Originally, the powers of the police jury included establishing a good police system, caring for levees and ditches, regulating public entertainment, and negotiating contracts. These powers were subsequently and substantially enlarged to encompass the ability to pass regulations promoting the peace, tranquility, security, or welfare of the parish.

Camille Zeringue served on the Jefferson Parish Police Jury during a period of time that saw many laws passed, including several that sought to control people of African descent, both slaves and free people of color. In the antebellum South, planters sought to control the lives of slaves in every way; legal sanctions were only one method by which planters sought dominion over those they considered their property. Among such laws passed by Zeringue and his fellow jurymen was one that forbade drinking or parties for slaves as well as any similar type of amusement. Another law forbade night dances in the slave cabins or huts on plantations. A letter was to be sent to all citizens concerning this ban.[13]

By outlawing such activities, Zeringue and his contemporaries acknowledged that such simple social ceremonies may have had deeper interpersonal implications. That is, while slave celebrations may seem like harmless social functions, elite whites realized that these events not only strengthened solitary and cohesiveness within the close-knit slave communities but also offered a prime opportunity for slaves to discuss and plan organized resistance efforts.

The Jefferson Parish Police Jury not only passed laws that sought to control slaves but also tightened regulations concerning free people of color. For example, one law aimed at the control of free people of color, which was passed by Camille Zeringue and his colleagues, made it illegal for any free person of color to host a party of ten or more people without the prior permission of a parish judge. The law stated that if a party was given without permission, the owner of the house in which the party was held would be fined $49, and, if the party was held outdoors, then each participant would be fined $5. The law also forbade slaves to attend such parties without their masters' written permission and established a fine of $10 for any slave who would violate this law. Finally, the law forbade any white person from participating in such a party (held by a free person of color) and established a $49 fine for any white person who did not comply with this law.

Although superficially Zeringue and his colleagues were afraid that such parties might get out of hand and cause some upheaval or disturbance, they were probably more concerned with the possibility of organized resistance aided by free persons of color that could result from such social gatherings. In addition, such laws functioned as a means of racial control, building a legal culture in which one race dominated the other.

By seeking to control the lives of slaves, planters like Zeringue brought even more power and control into their hands, preserving the social and economic order of the day. Ultimately, while the preservation of labor and, therefore, profits may have been the initial goal of such rigid control efforts, a more encompassing motivation soon developed. Planters like Zeringue sought to control their slaves and even free people of color simply because they believed such power was within their reach, further building a culture of coercion and supremacy.[14]

Under the rule of the new parish, Zeringue's plantation continued to prosper. Camille Zeringue married Madelein Lise Roman, daughter of Onisime Roman and Celeste Cantrelle, on June 6, 1827, shortly after the creation of Jefferson Parish. The Roman family was one of the most powerful, well known, and wealthiest plantation families in Louisiana. The family is still best known today for having constructed the mansion at Oak Alley Plantation, a house that has often been compared to the Zeringue mansion at Seven Oaks for its similar architectural plan, stylistic motif, and enormity. This union and others like it served not only to create a new family unit but also to consolidate plantation wealth and power, while strengthening the closed social world of plantation elite.

With this marriage, Madelein took on a new role, not only as a wife but also as plantation mistress. Of course, Camille Zeringue's mother still played an important role in plantation life, but Madelein was the planter's wife, and with this new identity came a large number of new responsibilities and duties. She was in charge of much more than just the plantation mansion. It was the mistress's obligation to oversee and regulate all domestic operations throughout the entire estate, including food preparation, clothing, and medical care. She was also in charge of both the physical and spiritual well being of her own family and of that of the slaves. Contrary to popular belief, plantation mistresses' duties were not confined to the mansion itself but extended from the kitchen to slave quarters and barns, a fact of life that Madelein learned quickly. Often problems arising on the plantation were brought directly to the mistress, bypassing the overseer's authority. In this way, plantation mistresses served as intermediaries between slaves and their masters, playing a pivotal role in the unique balance of power that existed within the realm of the southern plantation.[15]

Zeringue, his new wife, his siblings, and his mother continued to make their livelihood on Petit Desert plantation, which they now gave their name, the Zeringue Plantation. And it now was truly the Zeringue Plantation. In the time the family owned the plantation, it had grown from a mediocre plantation-farm to a very profitable estate, rivaling that of any of the neighbors along the great Mississippi River. Several generations of the Zeringue family later made their home at Seven Oaks—from Zeringue's mother to his children. The modern notion of the nuclear family (father, mother, and children) was not as heavily focused upon in antebellum times; rather, the extended family, often consisting of three of more generations and one or more family lines, was the core of home and family life.

Camille Zeringue relished his role as a planter, and he always explored ways to increase his prominence within the planter aristocracy. In the 1820s, he took on a leadership role in a crucial economic development. The Consolidated Planters Association was a land bank created in response to the relative lack of liquid capital available to Louisiana sugar planters. The association obtained $2,000,000 worth of English money from the British firm, Baring Brothers. The money was given in exchange for $7,740,200 of subscriptions that represented plantation mortgages. Only planters could purchase these subscriptions or shares, each valued at $500 (against their real estate). Camille Zeringue was among the first subscribers, initially purchasing 40 shares worth $20,000, and he was soon elected as one of the first members of the Association's board of directors. This role functioned to secure Zeringue's position within the economic realm of the planter elite. It gave him power over his fellow plantation owners and allowed him to guide the fiscal affairs of many of his neighbors.[16]

Zeringue happily and successfully made his living from his grand estate, and the transportation revolution that occurred after the invention of the steamboat meant even more power and success for him and his family. The first steamboat arrived at New Orleans in 1812, and by 1826 more than seven hundred steamboats traveled through the city. With the arrival of the first steamboat, the *New Orleans*, it was clear that this new mode of transportation was quite unique. With this change, New Orleans and surrounding areas experienced an unprecedented economic and cultural boom. Understanding the importance of the steamboat and the dramatic changes and growth it was causing for local planters and other businessmen, Camille Zeringue decided to embarked on a business venture that would ensure that he and his plantation benefited from this new transportation revolution.

In 1829, Camille Zeringue helped organize the Barataria and Lafourche Canal Company. The upper portion of the nearby Harang-Bouligny plantation had been purchased by Daniel Sparks and included a small canal, but Zeringue, along with fellow planters, envisioned a new, larger canal that would open waterways to steam vessels, making the area more accessible to vast markets and giving them greater control of waterway transportation.

The Barataria and Lafourche Canal Company was founded by Judge Charles Derbigny,[17] son of Louisiana governor Pierre Derbigny, and Walter Brashear, a surgeon originally from Kentucky. The original shareholders in the company included Camille Zeringue, L. LaBranche, Noël B. LeBreton, F. Fazend, Charles Derbigny, and Walter Brashear. The company received a charter from the state in 1829, and in the same year, Act 38, passed by the Louisiana legislature and signed by Governor Derbigny, afforded great benefits to the company.[18]

The company's capital stock, of $150,000 was divided into shares of $100 each. Originally, stocks would be sold by five commissioners appointed by the governor. Once these commissioners had sold six hundred shares, advertisements could be placed in local newspapers calling for the election of five company directors. The number of votes a stockholder was entitled to was to be proportional to the value of stock owned: one to five shares would confer one vote, with no stockholder, regardless of the value of his stock, to exceed ten votes. The directors to be elected were to serve the company without compensation. The board of directors of the Barataria and Lafourche Canal Company elected Charles Derbigny as president of the company; for this position, Derbigny received a salary.[19]

The new canal was to be designed with the steamboat in mind and had to be wide enough and deep enough for the passage of these great boats. The sight of the proposed canal belonged to Francois Enoul Livaudais; however, Camille Zeringue, certain of the coming success of the enterprise, persuaded investors to go upriver and construct the canal on his property. He gave the right-of-way, which was one arpent wide, through his plantation. Zeringue also gave permission for the use of half an arpent on either side of Bayou Segnette, which flowed on his property, as well as the rights of an existing smaller canal. The original agreement stated, "with right to cut trees as necessary to construct the locks of the canal which it proposes to cut through the land . . . as well as his rights on the canal which exists." Zeringue received forty shares of stock (then valued at $4,000) for his contribution to the company. He and his children were also rewarded free lifetime use of the canal.[20]

While his plantation's success had been steadily increasing, Zeringue sought to ensure his estate's future with the inclusion of the new canal. If the canal was a success, Zeringue knew that it would ultimately benefit him to have it on his property. Persuading investors to develop the canal on his plantation was a crafty, clever action. And, of course, the canal would play a prominent role in the life of the plantation throughout much of its remaining history.

The canal was probably built by greatly widening and deepening the smaller existing waterway. The new canal was constructed by both hand-labor and a dredging machine that consisted of an iron bucket on the front of a boat. The bucket is said to have operated by opening like a pair of bullet molds. This apparatus theoretically could dredge six hundred cubic yards a day but, in reality, it was much slower, averaging only about three hundred linear feet of finished canal each month.[21]

When completed, the new canal was thirty-seven feet wide and nine feet deep and ran from a curve in the Mississippi River through the Zeringue Plantation, where it connected with Bayou Segnette. It then continued west of Lake Salvador to Bayou LaFourche, providing a much-needed transportation route from New Orleans to the west.

The new canal dominated the Zeringue Plantation and provided Camille Zeringue with an immediate route of transportation with which few other planters could compete. Zeringue's plantation was situated near the interface of this large canal with the Mississippi River. Eventually locks were built. Various support structures and buildings (including slave cabins) were built along the canal, and, of course Zeringue continued to control land on both sides of the waterway. (See fig. 2.)

With the new canal opened, boats began making their way along it, providing the canal company a meager profit and the Zeringues a transportation route and a new communications corridor. The Barataria and Lafourche Canal Company was authorized to charge tolls. Vessels weighing less than a half-ton were to be charged fifty cents, while those weighing a half-ton or more were charged a dollar. Steamboats were given a 30 percent discount.[22]

Although private funds started the canal project, state funding was needed to continue operation. Considering the political connections of the canal's directors and stockholders, the state was more than enthusiastic in its support. The Louisiana legislature passed an act in 1833 giving the company a monopoly on canals to Bayou LaFourche and on rights to the ferries at either end. In 1835, the State of Louisiana purchased five hundred more shares of the company and provided slaves from the State Board of Internal Improvements for the canal's continued maintenance. In 1850, the canal company took out a $55,000 loan from the state. This loan was used to build the locks at the Mississippi River and at Bayou LaFourche. As a component of the loan agreement, the state received a mortgage on the entire canal.[23]

It is no surprise how willing state officials were to help this private company. Its owners were successful planters who controlled local economic and political affairs. One of the founders of the enterprise, Charles Derbigny, was the son of a former Louisiana governor who wrote the state's civil code. The other principal founder, Walter Brashear, was a state legislator. The other stockholders, Zeringue and his colleagues, were all wealthy sugar planters who wielded almost limitless political power and influence.

In the 1860 Slave Schedules, a supplement to the U.S. census of that year, the Canal Company was listed as owning eight slaves—six men and two women. Of these, one of the men was listed as a fugitive of the state. Maps from the time clearly show a few small cabins lined along the banks of the canal, near its intersection with the Mississippi River. (See fig. 2.)

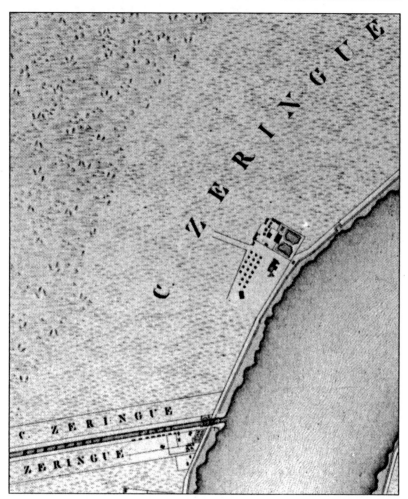

Fig. 2. Zeringue Plantation and the Company Canal. Map by Charles Zimpel, 1834 . This detailed map illustrates the layout of the Zeringue plantation before construction of the well-known mansion. The main plantation complex can be seen near the center of the image. Formal gardens are in front of the master house facing the Mississippi River. The building marked "Sh" is the sugar house that existed prior to the construction of the large sugar mill in the fields. The rows of slave cabins and a large building at the end of these rows, perhaps an overseer's house, are shown. A number of outbuildings and support structures are seen behind the master house. Lower in the image, the Barataria (Company) Canal is clearly marked, along with its locks. Zeringue owned property on both sides of the canal. There was also a row of possible slave cabins along one bank of the canal and other buildings near the locks. Courtesy of the Historic New Orleans Collection, accession no. 1955.19a detail.

The canal was ultimately sold to a group of investors from Houma and Thibodaux when the canal company was unable to make payments to the state. The investors, headed by Robert R. Barrow, took possession of the canal and adjacent property, including "locks with two gates, five double Negro cabins, one house, one office, one shed, one carpenter shop, eight slaves, one mule, one dray, and machinery."[24]

Despite new ownership, the canal continued to play a crucial role in the success of the Zeringue plantation, both before and after the Civil War. Its banks served as an encampment base for Confederate troops who built a fortification there. The canal later nurtured a unique and diverse community that grew along its banks.

CHAPTER THREE

The Zeringue Plantation House and Its Grounds

One might regard architecture as history arrested in stone.

—A. L. ROWSE, *The Use of History*

Architecture starts when you carefully put two bricks together.
There it begins.

—LUDWIG MIES VAN DER ROHE

Before the construction of their great mansion, the Zeringues lived in a small master house, which existed at the approximate location of the future residence. An 1823 inventory described this structure as "a master house about sixty feet square having eight rooms including two offices, bricked between posts with front and rear gallery, roofed with shingles." No known images of this house exist, although it can be seen on maps of the time. With their blossoming success, it soon became apparent to the family that the construction of a more fashionable home, one that would symbolize the family's own wealth and prominence and reflect the virility of the sugar industry in the state, should be undertaken.[1]

As the booming sugar industry brought unknown wealth into Louisiana, more and more sugar planters began to construct huge mansions for their families. Concurrently, Camille Zeringue was not only finding success with his sugar crop, as did his fellow planters, but was also reaping profits from the new canal he had organized. Empowered by this accomplishment, Zeringue sought to build an impressive mansion, in the then popular Greek Revival style that would mimic and, perhaps, surpass those homes of his equally wealthy neighbors. His, however, would have distinction.

Many sources agree that Camille Zeringue built the great Seven Oaks mansion for his widowed mother.[2] Clearly, he also built it with his wife and growing family in mind. The house was completed during the late 1830s or early 1840s. The Saulet House, on Annunciation Street in uptown New Orleans, boasts a very similar interior plan; it was completed in 1834.[3] The Oak Alley Plantation mansion in St. James Parish, whose exterior is similar to Seven Oaks, was built between 1837 and 1839.

No records exist that provide concrete evidence as to who designed or built the mansion at Seven Oaks, but it is clear that a well-schooled and dutiful architect was involved.[4] Some have argued that George Swainey, who built Oak Alley, may have also constructed Seven Oaks, because of the two houses' similar plans, overall designs, and scale. Others suggest that Francis D. Gott, who constructed the Waggaman Plantation house at Avondale under the supervision and designs of William Brand, built the mansion.[5] But, the most likely architect of the Seven Oaks mansion is Valentine von Werner. Zeringue family tradition points to this German architect as the designer of the mansion, and many sources agree.[6] Valentine von Werner, who was born in 1813 in Limberg-An-Der-Lahn, Germany, immigrated to New York, then later settled in New Orleans.[7] As an architect, he designed many structures and usually served as his own contractor, which he may have done for the Zeringue house. If this is so, it would cast doubt on the involvement of Gott or Swainey (as contractors) in the construction of the house. However, no firm evidence exists giving a clear answer to this question. Valentine von Werner continued working in New Orleans and the surrounding areas until his death in 1854.[8]

Whoever designed and built the home did so with much talent and aptitude. The Zeringue house is an excellent example of classic Greek Revival style. This architectural style swept widely over the region during this time period, and some examples remain today. But, at the same time, the house echoed unique Tuscan features that would set it apart from the many other mansions along the river. (See fig. 3.)

The mansion's nearly square form contained about 18 rooms and measured about 60 by 46.5 feet (not including porch, upper gallery, and columns). The house itself was raised from the porch and ground, requiring two steps at each of the fifteen ground-floor entrances. This feature created a mechanism that allowed air to circulate underneath the house

Fig. 3. The Zeringue mansion in all its glory. Photo courtesy of Charles Muller, Westwego, Louisiana.

(vents opened to the underside of the house) to aid in keeping the interior of the structure cool in the warm Louisiana climate.[9]

Eight huge Tuscan-style columns lined up against the front of the house, rising from the ground and extending above the second story. Both sides of the home boasted seven Tuscan columns identical to those in the front of the house, and the back, like the front, had eight huge columns. With each corner column, because of its position, simultaneously serving two sides, a total of twenty-six massive round brick columns, about eight feet apart, encircled the entire house.

These columns supported the huge slate roof and attic and provided room for the large balcony that completely surrounded the house and provided a covering above the ground-floor porch. The columns were constructed of solid pie-shaped brick wedges, imported from Europe, which builders fit together with mortar to create the great round shape. The wedges themselves were numbered so the builders would know how to fit them together. Each column was then covered with thick plaster to give it a smooth, gleaming white appearance. This building technique can be clearly seen in the photo of the deteriorating columns in the plantation's later days. The plaster had slowly disintegrated, exposing the rounded ends of the bricks. (See fig. 4.)

Fig. 4. This 1965 photo shows the mansion in deterioration. Much of the outside plaster has crumbled away from the columns. Pie-shaped bricks were used to build the inner core of the column structure, while curved bricks were placed concentrically around them. The bricks were manufactured in Europe and numbered so they could easily be assembled into columns. Photo by Richard Koch, courtesy of the Library of Congress, Prints & Photographs Division, HABS, Reproduction number HABS, LA, 26-WESWE, 1-10.

The columns supported the upper gallery or balcony, which surrounded the entire house. French doors from the upstairs bedrooms and the upper hall opened onto this open-air gallery. The floor of the gallery and the railings surrounding it were constructed from planks of Louisiana cypress, a hardy wood that resists termites. A lower gallery or porch also surrounded the entire house; builders lined it with flagstone, thought to have been imported by barge via the nearby Mississippi River. Such flagstone may have served as counterweights on barges and was accumulated as barges were unloaded and no longer required the counterweights. These individual flagstones were quite substantial in weight and volume, many being two or more inches thick and relatively wide and long. These stones were leveled in order to construct the veranda on top of a layer of river sand.

A large yet simple cornice supported the mansion's slate roof and attic, further mimicking traditional Tuscan style. Four symmetrical brick chimneys rose straight through the attic and emerged through the roof. These four chimneys carried smoke from thirteen fireplaces. Peeking gracefully from the slate roof, eight dormers, two on each of the four sides of the house, provided light to the massive attic, which may have been subdivided into smaller rooms. Above the eight dormers sat an open deck, also known as a widow's walk, with a balustrade that the Zeringues replaced with a belvedere (or cupola) during the Civil War.[10] Windows surrounded the belvedere, providing an excellent view of the Mississippi River and New Orleans. Because of the river's curve at this point, one could view the Mississippi River from almost any of the windows of the belvedere, no matter which direction they faced. Area planters would ascend above the attic into the belvedere to enjoy this wonderful view and watch ships and barges on the river. It also allowed Camille Zeringue a lookout point from which to survey his plantation and its activities, including the slaves and their labor.

Builders constructed both the interior and exterior walls from solid bricks and mortar. They then completely encased the interior walls in plaster. The exterior walls were covered with stucco for a finished look. Both the interior and exterior walls were 14 inches thick. Some evidence suggests that the bricks used in the construction of the mansion's walls may have been molded on site.[11]

The main entrance of the house originally faced the river.[12] The front entrance and the identical back entrance, as seen in the accompanied drawing, were true masterpieces of antebellum architectural detail. The rather large

(a)

Fig. 5(a–c). The doors of Seven Oaks Plantation. Front/back door, exterior doors, and interior doors. These drawings illustrate the attention to detail often associated with designing and constructing plantation houses such as Seven Oaks. Exterior doors, often mislabeled as French doors with shutters, were actually two sets of doors, the inner set with glass panes and the outer set of solid wood. Courtesy of Architect Davis Jahncke, New Orleans, Louisiana.

door was framed by an intricate medley of windows and millwork. Flat carved columns were topped by a heavy cornice. (See fig. 5a.)

As can be seen on the floor plan, the front doorway opened into a large formal entrance hall that extended into the center of the first floor. The entrance hall spanned a width of 15 feet. A set of French doors, similar to the doors of the entranceway, opened at the opposite side of the hall into the dining room—the largest room in the house. The dining room, which may have doubled as a ballroom, boasted a twenty-foot-high ceiling and measured

(b)

Fig. 5(b).

twenty by twenty-eight feet. Two fireplaces rested at opposite ends of the dining room. Mantels, made of fine black marble imported from Italy, framed the fireplaces. Opposite the door from the entrance hall, the dining room contained a door that opened onto the rear gallery. This door was framed on both sides by two smaller French casement doors.[13] (See fig. 5b.)

(c)

Fig. 5(c).

An early version of the ceiling fan, the "punkah," hung over the dining room table. Traditionally, a young slave boy would operate the punkah by pulling a string or rope attached to it. The punkah fanned the food in order to keep flies away and fanned the diners, who were often sweltering in the southern heat.[14]

Chimneys from the two fireplaces in the dining room rose to the second story. Because of their location and the plans of the two floors, if the chimneys were to have continued upward they would have extended through the center of the two rear upstairs bedrooms. Because of this problem, builders constructed the chimneys in a very unusual arrangement for this time period. They carried the chimneys across, in the wall and below the second floor. The chimneys then extended evenly and symmetrically through the second story, the attic, and finally through the roof.[15]

Two rooms sat on either side of the dining room. Camille Zeringue most probably used one of these as his office. The other room, which was similar in size, gave no firm indication of its original purpose, but could have served a variety of functions from a library to a servant's room. (See fig. 6a.)

Following the tradition of the time, the kitchen was not connected to the main house. Fear of fire, along with inadequate or nonexistent fire departments influenced this arrangement. The hot southern climate also prompted designers to create houses with kitchens separated from the main building.

The family often used the front of the first floor for receiving guests and entertaining, as well as for everyday use. Near the front of the house, two large rooms flanked the great entrance hall. Each of these rooms contained a fireplace. The family probably used them as parlors. Each measured twenty by eighteen feet. It was somewhat typical in French-influenced family mansions that certain rooms be reserved for gentlemen and others for ladies. It is likely that these two parlors served this function. When the Zeringues entertained, ladies could slip into their parlor to converse with one another away from the eyes and ears of the gentlemen, and, likewise, the men could enjoy smoking, drinking, and socializing in their parlor, where surely politics and planting were major topics of conversation.

Stairways stood behind each of these parlors. The stairway on the right led from the entrance hall to the second story and continued to the attic. It was thought to have been a private stairway for the family. The stairway on the left is thought to have been a service entrance because it led from the

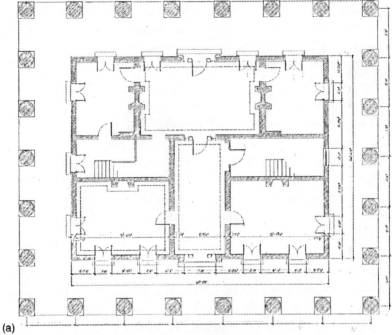

(a)

Fig. 6(a–b). These meticulously drawn floor plans illustrate the unique architectural features of Seven Oaks Plantation House. Note the central hallway ending in the large central dining room. The Zeringue family's private stairway is on the right, with an entrance from the main hall, while the stairway for the slaves (with entrance from outside) is on the left. The family's stairway continued to the third floor attic. Courtesy of Architect Davis Jahncke, New Orleans, Louisiana.

outside of the house to the upper stories, improving perhaps on Creole design themes that traditionally placed stairways outside the house. The small service stair hall also allowed for entrance from the outside porch directly into the dining room, which would have facilitated the delivery of food from the detached kitchen. Artisans constructed each of the stairways' banisters from solid mahogany. Under each of the stairways, builders tucked away a small room. One of these rooms may have served as a bath (under the family's stairwell), and the other room, under the servants' stairway, may have been used as a pantry or wine cellar.[16]

The second floor contained four bedrooms, each occupying a corner of the house. A large central hall extended from the front to the rear.[17] The central hallway measured fifteen feet wide by forty-five feet in length. Each bedroom was twenty by eighteen feet, and each boasted three exterior French

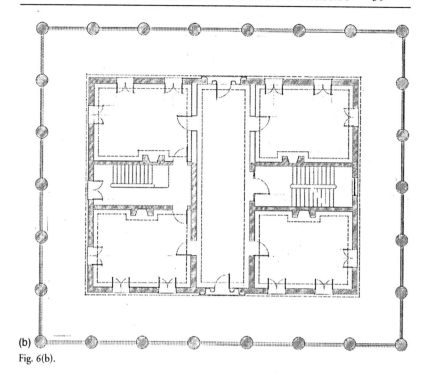

(b)

Fig. 6(b).

doors (one door on one wall and two on another), which opened onto the balcony surrounding the entire house, as is seen on the floor plan. (See fig. 6b.)

Above the second floor, eight dormers that surrounded the house (two on each of the four sides), illuminated the huge attic. The attic may have been divided into various rooms during the early life of the plantation. The house's four chimneys rose symmetrically from the second floor straight through the massive attic. Pegs joined the heavy roof rafters and beams that supported the slate roof. In the center of the attic, a winding staircase led to the belvedere. Contemporary Zeringue family oral tradition indicates that this winding staircase was at one time lined with mirrored panels. This is said to have created a magnificent entrance way to the "fourth floor" belvedere.

The entire house contained only two actual windows, in addition to those in the belvedere and attic. The two windows were located along the family stairway. Twenty-six sets of exterior French doors located throughout the house, made up for the lack of windows. The doors were constructed of solid wood at the bottom and contained eight panes of glass at the top. An exterior set of solid wooden doors protected each set of French doors. Servants bolted the solid doors closed from the inside during a storm or hurricane in order to protect the house and the inhabitants inside. The house also contained four solid wooden exterior doors that did not share their openings with French doors and contained no glass panes.[18]

The overall plan of the mansion was a unique hybrid of Creole and Anglo architecture. These two social groups, who made up the aristocracy of Louisiana's sugar empire, often clashed in their social and political ideals, but occasionally their architectural styles merged. The Zeringue mansion represented one of the most complete fusions of these two architectural traditions. For example, the plan of most so-called Creole mansions included exterior French doors surrounding a building with no central hallway, whereas Anglo structures often featured Georgian plans with large central hallways running the length of the houses with two rooms flanking each side. The Zeringue home contained both of these elements. French doors, often associated with Creole structures, opened around the house, allowing for access to the Anglo-inspired wraparound gallery and balcony. The most striking meld of the architectural traditions is the grand hall. Central in location, this hallway was obviously inspired by the popular Georgian plan, but an abrupt end near the center of the mansion, an opening into a centrally placed dining room, is unusual. The location of the dining room represents adherence to Creole design; therefore, the hallway's end in the middle of the house was a perfect union of both prominent architectural influences.[19]

Stylistically, builders constructed the Zeringue house on harsh lines and added no fancy decorations or embellishments. The house needed none of the gaudy embellishments used by other plantation houses of the time; its massiveness and strength provided all that was needed to create a sense of awe in the eyes of all who gazed upon it. The house functioned to communicate the family's ultimate status in society and to represent its dominance over the people who they enslaved.

Outside the house, on one side, was a huge cistern, a necessary external addition to any plantation house, as potable drinking water was an obvious requirement. Rainwater was collected from the roof via large spouts that ran directly into the cypress barrel-like reservoir. At other smaller buildings on the plantation actual barrels (often the same hogsheads used to store sugar) were used as functional cisterns.

Surrounding the mansion outside, formal gardens can clearly be seen on Zimple's 1834 map of the area.[20] As was customary, much care was taken to create formal gardens which were truly showcases. Many planters spent much time and effort in planning and laying out their gardens. Precision in this area was considered a virtue, and some planters even paid professional gardeners to ensure that their gardens would be the envy of their neighbors in the mansions along the great Mississippi River.[21] (See fig. 2.)

Originally, many other structures surrounded the house and gardens. The plantation was clearly laid out in the "nodal-block" style, with rows of buildings filing behind one another to create a gridlike pattern of structures.[22]

At least twenty-two slave cabins stood about four hundred feet from the main house. Several maps of the area, including an 1872 map found in the New Orleans Notarial Archives, show that these cabins were arranged in about five parallel rows in village-like fashion, further echoing the traditional nodal-block layout of the plantation. Such cabins were usually sectioned off from the area of the main house by a planting of trees.[23] (See fig. 7.)

Slave cabins were generally crude wooden structures, but, despite their appearances, they were very functional houses. In the sugar parishes, it was common for slave cabins to be "small Creole quarter houses," similar in type to the typical raised Creole cottage with a large, tall roof overhanging a built-in porch. It is likely that this was the type of cabins seen on the Zeringue plantation, given that they are most common in the sugar region and that similar structures can be found on neighboring estates.[24]

The typical slave cabin was about sixteen by eighteen feet but ranged in size. In Louisiana, it was customary for two families (often with many children) to share one of these small houses. On the Zeringue estate, there were on average four or five slaves per cabin, but there is no indication of how families or individuals were assigned cabins; that is, it is somewhat unclear whether each cabin held a similar number of slaves.[25]

Inside the slave cabin could be found a few pieces of simple furniture: a mattress made of Spanish moss, a wooden table, and a few chairs. There were no closets; slaves hung their few pieces of clothing on a nail in the wall. There were open windows with no glass panes but with wooden shutters that could be closed for protection from the cold and rain.[26]

Around these sparse cabins, Camille Zeringue would have allowed slaves to have their own garden plots in order to raise vegetables to supplement

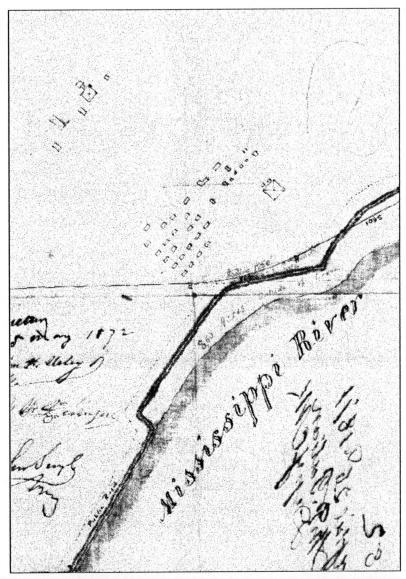

Fig. 7. An 1872 Map of the Zeringue Plantation. By 1872, the layout of the Zeringue plantation had changed from previous decades. Prior to the Civil War, the sugar house and associated support structures were relocated into the fields, some distance behind the main plantation complex. By this time the mansion was complete, as indicated at the front of the plantation near the Mississippi River. Kitchens, barns, and other buildings were located behind the master house. The slave cabins retained their overall configuration and location as noted on Zimple's 1834 map. Theodore Guyol, May 25, 1872. Courtesy of the New Orleans Notarial Archives.

their rations.[27] Each slave family usually tended its own garden, which produced a variety of vegetables. Additionally, most slaves were allowed to hunt and fish in the wilderness and wetlands surrounding the plantation. This provided slaves with added variety in their diets along with an opportunity to earn spending money through the trade of fish, meat, and animal hides.[28] Mary Reynolds, who spent many years as a slave in Louisiana, described her family's small garden plot:

> "Sometimes massa let niggers have a li'l patch. They'd raise taters or goobers [peanuts]. They liked to have them to help fill out on the victuals. Taters roasted in the ashes was the best tastin' eatin' I ever had. I could die better satisfied to have jus' one more tater roasted in hot ashes. The niggers had to work the patches at night and dig the taters and goobers at night. Then if they wanted to sell any in town they'd have to git a pass to go. They had to go at night, cause they couldn't ever spare a hand from the fields."[29]

While most historians have focused on the master's central role in constructing the built environment of the plantation, it has been suggested that enslaved person's themselves influenced the environment of the plantation. Surely the Zeringue slaves, like others in their situation, exerted influence in the area of the cabins and throughout the plantation where they worked and lived, and may have done so as a subtle act of resistance. Something as simple as a dirt path through a thick wooded area could have served a great social function, allowing communication between neighboring plantations or providing a route to a secret meeting place. Such subtle modifications upon the land, however, have long been reclaimed by nature.[30]

Slave cabins were not the only structures to surround the Zeringues' great house. Among the many structures was a house or cabin for visiting priests. In an 1852 letter to Father Stephen Rousselon, Sister Aliquot, a Roman Catholic nun who periodically resided on the plantation with the Zeringue family, described an altar at the plantation that Father F. Zeller had built for celebrating mass. Zeringue and his family were devout Catholics, and Zeringue asked the Archbishop of New Orleans to send sick priests to him in order for them to be rejuvenated by the wholesome plantation air.[31] It was Zeringue's dream to build a grand chapel on his estate; however, the dream was apparently never realized.[32]

In addition to the houses and cabins, there were many other important structures throughout the plantation grounds. As can be seen on the 1872 map of the plantation, about 160 feet behind the Zeringues' main house, workers built about ten structures that were used as various shops and stables. And, at some time, a sugar mill and purgerie were constructed, both located about 1,200 feet away from the house. The sugar mill was where sugarcane was processed into granular sugar; it was the factory of the plantation and the heart of production. It was usually a massive structure that, when in operation, buzzed with activity and excitement. The purgerie was a building where barrels of sugar were drained of molasses in the final step before granulated sugar was ready for sale. (See fig. 7.) Sugar could be sold domestically or shipped to Europe; either way, the planters stood to make a great profit!

Great profits had not always been associated with sugar. Sugarcane first arrived in Louisiana about 1750, when Jesuit priests in Santo Domingo shipped the crop to their fellow Jesuits in New Orleans. The Jesuits grew and harvested this sugarcane on property located in the present downtown area. The cane was not grown for the granulation of sugar; instead the sweet, chewable stalks were marketed as confections to the citizens of New Orleans.[33]

It was not until the late 1700s, that sugar, produced from sugarcane, became an important commodity. In 1794, Étienne de Boré built an open kettle sugar mill on his plantation, located in present-day Audubon Park in uptown New Orleans. The next year, de Boré showcased his mill to local planters, who were astounded to see that he had successfully granulated sugar from sugarcane. De Boré is often given more credit than he deserves: many claim he was the first successfully to granulate sugar, but this process had been going on for hundreds of years elsewhere. Regardless, he first realized the magnitude of profits that could be made from sugar production in Louisiana, and he shared this enthusiasm with his fellow planters.

In the narrative of experiences as a slave on Louisiana cotton and sugar plantations, Soloman Northup describes how a typical sugar mill on a large Louisiana plantation appeared: "The mill is an immense brick building, standing on the shore of the bayou. Running out from the building is an open shed, at least an hundred feet in length and forty or fifty feet in width."[34] The sugar mill, purgerie, and slave cabins were among the most utilized buildings surrounding the grand plantation mansion. From the mansion's high cupola, the Zeringues could survey a complete network of outbuildings, warehouses, workshops, and storage structures. These were necessary, as life on the plantation was comprised not only of planting and harvesting but also of producing and maintaining everything needed for this almost completely self-sufficient community.

Chapter Four

Life and Agricultural Production on the Zeringue Plantation

It is a maxim universally agreed upon in agriculture, that nothing must be done too late; and again, that everything must be done at its proper season; while there is a third precept which reminds us that opportunities lost can never be regained.

—Pliny the Elder (c. 23 A.D.–79 A.D.)

Perhaps no life was more independent than that of a Southern planter before the late war.

—Susan Dabney Smedes, *Memorials of a Southern Planter*

Life on the plantation was good for the Zeringue family. Their plantation, like those of their prosperous neighbors, was for the most part a completely self-sufficient community, over which the family, led by Camille, had near complete dominion. A mid-nineteenth-century Louisiana plantation the size of Seven Oaks was a farm and factory but also encompassed much more. The plantation produced everything from vegetables, fruits, eggs, milk, poultry, and pork to candles, wool, and leather. The surrounding wooded areas provided game for food and furs, wood for fuel and lumber, raw materials for the manufacture of brick, and even shells for making whitewash. The river and nearby wetlands provided an abundance of seafood: fish, shrimp, crabs, and shellfish. In 1860, in addition to his principal sugar crop, Zeringue produced 7,800 bushels of Indian corn (much more than his fellow planters in Jefferson

Parish), 150 bushels of Irish potatoes, and 100 bushels of sweet potatoes, most of which was probably consumed on his plantation. In addition, Zeringue owned twice as many horses and nearly twice as many milch cows compared to the median among the large slaveholders of Jefferson Parish.[1] The plantations of the Louisiana sugar parishes were also noted for producing butter, hay, orchard fruits, honey, beeswax, tobacco, rye, wine, wheat, hops, barley, clover, grass seed, cheese, millet, and rice.[2]

A variety of skilled workers were also on the Zeringue plantation. Often, slaves trained to be carpenters, blacksmiths, or masons, thereby holding special positions in the plantation community. Their masters relied on them and other such skilled workers because of their unique talents. Self-sufficiency was highly prized among the Louisiana planters and their contemporaries throughout the South. It is said that Valcour Aime, a wealthy planter of St. James Parish, won a ten-thousand-dollar bet by serving a dinner in which everything—fish, game, fruits, nuts, coffee, cigars, and wine—was supplied from his estate.[3] Such self-sufficiency and independence gave plantations, and the planters who owned them, a great deal of autonomy. This is not to suggest that the master, his family, and even the slaves, did not rely on some things produced outside of the plantation boundaries. The smaller a plantation, the less self-sufficient it was. The Zeringues would have certainly gone to New Orleans occasionally to purchase ready-made goods produced domestically or imported from Europe. They would have probably taken their own boat or ridden the ferry across the river, and once the steamboat became commonplace, they may have availed themselves of that luxury.

But, of the variety of things produced in the self-sufficient plantation community, in the mind of Camille Zeringue and his fellow planters, sugar was, of course, the most important commodity to come from the vast estate. By the early nineteenth century, national demand for sugar was so great it could not be adequately satisfied. With such a demand, the price of sugar soared. Its success further aided by a U.S. tariff, the Louisiana sugar industry boomed.

In order to provide sugar for the demanding market and in order to provide maximum profits for the planter, sugar production was the top priority on the Zeringue plantation and other sugar plantations of southeastern Louisiana. The process of producing sugar began with planting cane, and the majority of slaves on a sugar plantation found themselves working primarily in the fields.

After harvesting, cane was transported to the sugarhouse, the center point of the entire sugar plantation operation, which contained the mill that turned cane into sweet, white sugar. The Zeringues' earliest sugar mill was surely an open-kettle-type mill, in which large kettles were used to granulate sugar. This early sugarhouse can clearly be seen on an 1834 map of area. It is marked "Sh" for sugarhouse and sits near the master house and slave cabins.

In years to come, mechanical and technological innovations of the day transformed the Zeringues' old open kettle mill into a steam-powered, machine-operated factory. But, despite technological innovations, the production of sugar was still a labor-intensive process that relied heavily on the institution of slavery to provide all of the physical labor. In the 1840s and 1850s, vacuum pans were installed on larger plantations, including that of Camille Zeringue.

In 1844, a free man of color, Norbert Rillieux, invented a process in which steam from one vacuum pan could be used over and over to heat another vacuum pan. The Rillieux Apparatus, as it came to be known, represented a major technological breakthrough compared to the earlier open kettle mills. It was the open kettle process, as mentioned earlier, that had been utilized by the Zeringues, but once the Rillieux Apparatus became available, Zeringue ushered his sugar production into the technological age.

The old sugarhouse on the plantation was replaced by a new, much larger structure to accommodate this novel machinery. The new sugarhouse was moved far back, behind the mansion and slave cabins, into the fields. This moved production on the plantation directly into the region where the cane was grown and allowed Zeringue to minimize the distance he had to transport his raw cane. This was essential, because as soon as the cane was cut from the fields it had to be transported to the sugarhouse for grinding as quickly as possible as the sucrose content of the cane quickly began to deteriorate after being cut.

The process of transporting sugarcane from the fields to the plantation's sugar mill was more arduous than can be imagined. Without motorized vehicles, most planters relied on oxen- or mule-pulled carts to complete the task. This, however, was not always effective as overloaded carts often got stuck in the mud, broke an axle, or encountered a host of other problems causing delays. In later years, some planters began to ship their cane to the mill by placing it on barges to float it downriver or along one of the plantation's drainage canals. Once trains became a standard form of transportation, some planters installed complex closed-track railroads that ran throughout the plantation for this purpose as well. Zeringue may have had such a system at his plantation, because court records indicate he sold a steam engine. By moving his sugarhouse Zeringue ensured a swift trip to the mill for his cane and a minimum of transportation hassles.

Moving the sugarhouse also had a wider social meaning: it ensured that industrialized production and all of the unpleasantries that went with it were separated from the mansion and domestic life there. The process of producing sugar from cane, especially during the hectic grinding season,[4] was certainly chaotic and brought with it a multitude of work and a number of disagreeable sights and foul odors. By moving the sugarhouse far away from his home, Zeringue defined the mansion as an oasis from the realities of production for himself and his family.

P. A. Champomier reported in an annual listing of sugar production in Louisiana, that Zeringue produced three hundred hogsheads[5] of sugar using the Rillieux Apparatus during the 1849–50, season. Such a production, not considering other crops and investments, ensured that the family lived a comfortable life. In the years since their mansion had been constructed, mechanical innovations had allowed the Zeringues to streamline many of their agricultural and productive operations to guarantee maximum success for the plantation and the family. By 1860, the Zeringues continued to produce 300,000 pounds of sugarcane along with 18,000 gallons of molasses as a by-product of that sugar production.[6]

Once cane from the fields was produced into saleable sugar, Camille Zeringue began planning one of the most crucial steps in the process—marketing his sugar crop. "The conversion of the crop into cash" was an extremely important step in the process of running a successful sugar plantation. This was usually accomplished by shipping the sugar to New Orleans by steamboat where it would be sold to the highest bidder by a paid commission merchant or factor on a levee platform or by selling the sugar on the plantation wharfs along the river.[7]

Whereas sugar was the primary cash crop grown by Camille Zeringue, evidence suggests cotton was grown on the plantation as well. After the

Civil War, a cotton gin was among items seized from the Zeringues by Union forces. This was not unusual as cotton had become the most success-ful staple crop in the South by the mid-nineteenth century. The role cotton played for the Zeringue plantation could have been as meager as a small crop produced for local use or as mighty as a large cash crop grown for export. Either way, cotton production was a way of life on the Zeringue plantation and throughout the South. Cotton's amazing domination and success as an export crop had completely enlivened the economy of the South and had functioned to boost further the importance of New Orleans as a major city and port.[8]

The boom in the cotton and sugar industries that succeeded in cementing a firm southern economy and strengthening southern solidarity also changed everyday life for the Zeringues and their contemporaries. Life in Louisiana was always influenced by its French and Spanish past, but American influ-ences now affected life as well. By the nineteenth century, the plantation South was flourishing, and, in Louisiana, a strong culture emerged rooted in European ideology and customs, while embracing the benefits of American nationalism. The Zeringues were the epitome of this rich blend, as they con-tinued practicing European ways so engrained in the hearts and minds of the Louisiana citizenry (even speaking French and following European customs) while benefiting from American economic and social ideology.

Surrounded by vast fields of sugarcane and cotton, Camille Zeringue and his wife, Madelein Lise Roman, raised their children in the great man-sion on their plantation. The 1850s census of Jefferson Parish lists Camille Zeringue, age fifty-nine, occupation "planter," and his wife, Lise, age forty. At this time, the value of real estate owned by Zeringue was listed at $80,000 (an amount equal to about $1.6 million in the year 2000).[9] The Zeringues are said to have had eight children.[10] Seven are listed in the cen-sus of 1850: three sons, Michael, age eighteen; Fortuné, age fourteen; and Edmond, age ten; and four daughters, Camille, age sixteen; Adeline, age twelve; Lise, age eight; and Celeste, age five.[11]

The census indicated that the younger children, Fortuné, Adeline, Edmond, Lise, and Celeste, all attended school that year. At age eleven, the children began their formal education, following tightly scheduled and reg-ulated lesson plans. A Creole tutor from Martinique, who spoke both

French and English fluently, resided on the plantation to teach the children, but the children's early religious instruction was handled by their mother. Madelein felt that only she could provide the depth of religious instruction she desired for her children, so she tutored them in the catechism regularly. When old enough, the girls were independently sent to a boarding school run by the Sisters of the Sacred Heart, where they made their first communions and confirmations.[12]

The census of 1850, further reveals that Camille Zeringue's eighteen-year-old son, Michael, worked for his father as an overseer. The job was no easy task. In this capacity, Michael was the second-in-command of the entire plantation and all its operations. He was also directly in charge of his father's slaves, which then numbered over a hundred. The Zeringue plantation was highly organized with a strict chain of command, and Michael would have been second only to his parents, the plantation master and mistress. In his book, *Louisiana Sugar Plantations During the Civil War*, Charles P. Roland compares the complex plantation hierarchy to that of a military organization: "Slave organization has been compared with that of an army. The master was the commander, and the overseer his lieutenant. From the overseer the chain of command ran through first and second drivers, who performed the functions of sergeants, to the common hands—the private soldiers of the slave company. The plantation bell was to the Negroes what the bugle is to troops. It was rung in the morning by the first driver as the quarter's reveille; meals were announced by its tolling; and at night it sounded taps to send the laborers to their cabins."[13]

As the overseer of his father's plantation, Michael assembled the slaves each morning and assigned them daily duties. He was also in charge of slave discipline. Often such discipline took the form of the whip but could range from milder punishments, such as the revocation of privileges, to much harsher consequences such as branding. No hard evidence exists to suggest where Michael or his father may have fallen on this continuum of cruelty, but period records from the point of view of Zeringue's daughters (which themselves are obviously biased to some degree) do tend to suggest that the Zeringues were relatively mild masters.[14]

Aside from disciplining the slaves, Michael supervised the personal hygiene and health of the slaves and arranged for the sick to receive proper medical care. Slaves represented a large investment for the master, so care of the ill was given top priority. Many large plantations even boasted their own on-site hospitals, but it is not known whether the Zeringues had such a facility at Seven Oaks.

Aside from these duties, Michael was also responsible for seeing that the slave quarters and cottages were kept in an orderly fashion. He was required to do bed checks several times a week and to account for the slaves' whereabouts. If a slave wished to leave the plantation (for example, in order to visit another plantation), he first had to obtain permission from the overseer, who usually gave the slave a written pass. Likewise, a visiting slave from another plantation first had to apply for entry with the overseer, usually presenting a pass from his or her own overseer.

Additionally, as overseer, Michael was responsible for the drivers who were slaves in positions of power over other slaves. Drivers were chosen from among the slaves. Masters looked for those with the greatest intelligence and leadership abilities to assume this important role.[15] They were responsible for supervising all slaves' labor, including labor in the fields. The drivers were also charged with checking the slave quarters and exercising disciplinary action over other slaves when necessary. The position of the driver was a unique one, filled with paradox. Even though a driver was a superior to the field hands and other slaves, he was himself a slave.[16]

Aside from disciplining fellow slaves and supervising labor on the plantation, the chief driver or "first driver" was also required to report to the overseer each morning. Michael would have taken this (usually verbal) account, which contained information about the slaves and the daily activities of the plantation, and then made his own concise written or verbal report to his father, the plantation master.

The position of overseer was one that required great patience, common sense, and a dynamic personality. He was often said to have been treated by the master and master's family with simultaneous courtesy and condescension.[17] Certainly, Camille and his wife did not look on their son with condescension, but as Michael took the position as overseer he also stepped into a new role in the family and plantation dynamics. How exactly Michael juggled the roles of both son and overseer may never be known, but surely at times the two roles overlapped and at other times even conflicted.

In any area of plantation operations it was Camille Zeringue, the master and planter, who held the absolute authority. Some have compared nineteenth-century planters to barons and other landholding aristocrats of Europe. Though there are significant differences in the two groups, they have one thing in common: landownership. And like the manors of Europe, the antebellum plantation was in many ways an entirely self-sufficient community, ruled autonomously by the plantation master.

To work such vast lands, the planter relied heavily on his enslaved labor force, a class of people held by the master as his legal property. Early colonial planters exploited enslaved people simply for their labor, but, by antebellum times, a different situation had arisen. Planters, like Zeringue, took a paternalistic role in their relationships with their slaves, which was partially the product of society's moral and ethical question of how one human being could rightfully own another. Gradually, slave owners began to voice their seemingly altruistic feelings of how much they "cared" for their "poor" slaves. This paternalism manifested itself in several unique ways. As slaveholders became more and more interested in the lives of their chattel, they began to envision themselves as generous patriarchs.[18]

The plantation became akin to an immense family in which the planter viewed himself as the wise, charitable father and his slaves as inferior, irrational, and impudent children. Regardless of the sincerity of this attitude, by the time Zeringue took control of his family's plantation, paternalism had taken root in the slaveholding South. Paternalism became so engrained in southern culture, some masters actually convinced themselves, on one level or another, that by enslaving individuals they were actually providing a charitable service. None was more passionate in his role as "great father" of the plantation than Zeringue. In the biographies of their lives, his daughters recounted that their plantation was indeed a family, ruled by their father, and that the slaves were treated like his own children.

Having his own son Michael running the day-to-day operations of the plantation as overseer gave Camille Zeringue the opportunity to focus on diversions and other activities, but it is most likely that he kept a keen eye on his business at all times and an active hand in the lives of his slaves. One activity that Zeringue participated in outside his plantation was bidding at auctions. Records show that on December 22, 1855, Zeringue attended an auction where he bid on a pair of bay carriage horses, which were brought for sale at the auction by Jonas Pickles, a resident of New Orleans. The horses were approximately eight years old and "well broken to double or single harness." A handwritten note from Pickles accompanied the horses. It requested that the auctioneer, George May, sell the horses without guarantee. The note assured the auctioneer that although the horses were to be sold without guarantee, they were sound animals.[19]

Little did Zeringue know his innocent bidding would lead to a great deal of worry and concern soon after. Zeringue made the highest bid for the two horses—$310. He paid $100 of the debt up front. Only a day later Pickles sent a note to Zeringue requesting he pay the remainder of his debt. After examining the horses, Zeringue found their condition to be more than questionable. He found one of the horses to be afflicted with vertigo, a disease commonly known at that time as "blind staggers." Zeringue refused to pay the remainder of the debt and refused as well to take the horses. He argued that blind staggers caused the horse to be dangerous and therefore worthless.[20]

Jonas Pickles sued Camille Zeringue for a total of $255, which included the $210 that was still remaining from the original bid and an additional $45 for feeding and boarding the animals. Zeringue and his legal counselors answered the suit in a document that stated: "this defendant was willing to purchase [the horses] for the use of his family had they been such as they were represented to be, but the contrary being the fact your respondent [argues] that the action of the plaintiff is a gross attempt to defraud this respondent and to extract money from him without an equivalent which can receive no countenance from this honorable court."[21]

While in court, Pickles produced several witnesses, including Thomas L. McGhee. McGhee had originally sold Pickles these two horses and testified that neither had vertigo. He further stated that the only affliction that one of the horses suffered was a problem with its foot. McGhee stated that the horse's foot was bruised, causing it to shed its hoof, but that when the hoof grew back, the horse was perfectly well. He estimated the total value of the pair of horses to be between $500 and $700, although he sold the pair to Pickles for a sum between $400 and $450.[22]

A second witness, Frank Cannon, was brought onto the stand. Cannon was an employee of Pickles' who worked as a warehouseman. It was Cannon who received the horses from McGhee and delivered them to Pickles. Cannon testified that he had driven the horses often and never knew them to run away. He did remark that one would often shy away in developed areas because he was not accustomed to towns. Cannon stated that at the auction he heard George May, the auctioneer, state: "this is a pair of fine carriage horses. They have to be sold just as they stand. What will you give for them?"[23] Under cross-examination, Cannon's testimony aided the defense when he was unable to say whether the horses were sold in sound condition or not, even though he had attended the auction.

A ruling stated: "Under such the facts [the plaintiff, Jonas Pickles] can not expect that a court of Justice will assist him in defrauding the defendant in this case. It is therefore ordered adjudged and decreed that there be judgment for defendant and that plaintiff's demand [be] dismissed . . . rendered April 15, 1856."[24]

With that, the case of *Jonas Pickles vs. Camille Zeringue* was settled—the court having decided in Zeringue's favor. Zeringue put this case behind him and continued with his successful plantation business. The case was historically very enlightening for a number of reasons. It further confirmed the type of person Zeringue was: domineering and influential. Like the Holmes and Parsons case, it also provided clues pertaining to the planter culture of the area. Even though the evidence in the case seems to favor Zeringue, the idea of a successful planter being manipulated by a man like Jonas Pickles was not taken lightly by the highly stratified society of antebellum Louisiana. Zeringue was a powerful, well-known aristocrat, active in local politics, and, as such, his influence and the influence of the cultural norms that predominated were felt far and wide, even throughout the judicial branches of government.

In contrast to the Holmes and Parsons case that lingered for several years, the verdict in this suit was rendered in a swift and unquestioned manner. This may have simply been an artifact of a more clear-cut case or lighter docket for the court, or perhaps a deeper, more subtle meaning can be inferred. In the late 1820s and early 1830s when Camille Zeringue sued Eleazor Holmes and Joseph Parsons over their failure to pay him for a steam engine, his identity as a planter had already been established; however, by 1856, this identity was firmly and definitely secured in the business and social community and wider body politic. Also, during the Holmes and Parsons case, the Zeringues made their home in the smaller house that preceded their great mansion, but by the time Jonas Pickles filed suit, Zeringue and his family were established in their impressive mansion, which certainly functioned to communicate the family's wealth, power, and place in society. Perhaps the contrasting length of time between the initial suit and verdict in favor of this planter in these two different cases actually coincides with Zeringue's own personal rise to the top echelon of the planter elite and the tightly intertwined success of his plantation.

Zeringue's prominence among his powerful planter peers developed and blossomed over time much like his plantation. Also, the family's station similarly developed in the highly organized antebellum culture of French-dominated Louisiana.[25] They became more prominent as their plantation prospered and remained on their property the ultimate sovereigns.

Life on the nearly autonomous plantation was, for the Zeringues, a privileged existence. The family lived in the opulent splendor of their mansion, their financial and social lives stable and secure. During the social season, the family attended a variety of balls and parties. Social life was extremely important for the planter and his family. Aside from simply attending such events, the family surely hosted many parties and balls. The mansion's immense first floor—with its parlors, large hall, and large dining room—was specifically designed for entertaining. Living so close to New Orleans, the Zeringues were also likely to have hosted a number of overnight guests at their home, often when friends and associates from the city sought solace from hectic city life. It is said that the hospitality of the region was almost without limits. Nearly every weekend the grand plantations surrounding New Orleans were filled with visitors and guests. Many enjoyed hunting in the vast and untamed wilderness surrounding the estates. They also occupied their time playing cards, dining, singing, and dancing. It was not unusual for these weekend getaways to extend over several weeks or even months, but the hospitality of the master and his family seldom dwindled.[26]

The head of this hospitable antebellum plantation family was, of course, the father, Camille Zeringue, who was the ideal model of the typical antebellum father. In her book *Daily Life in Louisiana, 1815–1830*, Liliane Crété iterates what that ideal model encompassed: "His word was law, his judgment final and without appeal. Yet the Creole paterfamilias was far from abusing his privileges: he was notoriously an affectionate and indulgent parent and a generous and loving husband, through not always a scrupulously faithful one."[27]

Camille Zeringue was not only the typical antebellum father but also the ideal of the southern planter. A dominant businessman and leader in his community, he fit the profile perfectly. The life of a planter was extremely independent, only answering to the whims of the weather and the market. Crété further elucidates the life of the planter: "The wealthy Creole planter ruled his estate like an absolute monarch; his subject, the slaves, were expected to minister to his slightest desire. His style of living was a mirror of his prosperity: the large house, large family, great expanse of cotton or sugarcane, orchard and vegetable garden to supply his table, and ornamental garden laid out on a grand scale, bright with rare and beautiful flowers. His highest ambition for his children was that they might emulate his own style of living. He considered that all change was for the worse and contemplated the past with more pleasure than the future."[28]

Zeringue was also a dynamic, driven man with much ambition and zest for life. In the short biographies of their lives, Zeringue's daughters remembered how their father would often get involved in their favorite hobby: artificial flower making. As a planter, Zeringue was quite mobile and left the plantation regularly to do business or hunt. When he returned, he often brought some exotic variety of wildflower, which he would dare his daughters to replicate. Enlivened by the challenge, the girls scoured the plantation for feathers, seeds, fish scales, and other accessible materials. They skillfully and tediously produced an accurate artificial version of the flower. The girls were taught this craft by their mother, who also excelled at it. They continued this unique hobby throughout their lives.

Of course, the Zeringue family members were not the only residents of the plantation. Certainly, they were indeed the most powerful and prominent inhabitants, and it is their story that is often remembered in accounts and records. But the Zeringues represented only a fraction of the plantation's many residents. The powerful labor force that drove the massive production on the plantation was the slaves who made their humble dwellings in the shadow of the great mansion. In the 1860 Slave Schedule, a supplement to the federal census of that year, Zeringue was listed as the owner of 108 slaves. Seventy of these slaves were males from eight to seventy-six years old. Of the remaining thirty-eight females, six were one year old and the oldest was fifty-eight. The records also report that Camille Zeringue owned twenty-three slave houses on the plantation.

As a planter who owned more than fifty slaves, Zeringue was listed as one of the "large slaveholders." According to the 1860 census, the average number of slaves held by "large slaveholders" in Jefferson Parish was 107.[29] Throughout the data, the numbers are somewhat skewed because of one slaveholder with unusually high values (H. C. Millaudon[30]), but when noting a more robust figure, the median number of slaves held by these planters is 91. Zeringue's holdings remain well above those of the majority of the largest slaveholders in the parish. Likewise, when noting the median cash value of farms belonging to the largest slaveholders in Jefferson Parish, we see that Zeringue's farm, at $90,000, is well above the median of $80,000. Furthermore, while the average number of slaves per dwelling throughout the estates of the large slaveholders of Jefferson Parish was 5.05, the average number of slaves per dwelling on the Zeringue estate was 4.65, a fact that may indicate that the Zeringue slaves faced slightly better conditions, or at least less crowding in their cabins.[31]

Zeringue's slaves had virtually no rights and were literally at the mercy of their master. Life on a sugar plantation was extremely difficult for these slaves not only because they were considered and treated as racial, social, and legal subordinates but because of the grueling labor associated with the production of sugar and the harsh physical conditions of southeastern Louisiana.

Many enslaved people transcended the great horrors of their bondage through their faith and religious practices. In this realm, however, the Zeringues tried to control the lives of their slaves. Zeringue and his family were devout Roman Catholics, as were many of the white families of the region. Zeringue was active in the church, even offering the use of his plantation to the archbishop as a retreat for sick priests, as he thought that the fresh air would be good for their health. Unlike many Protestant slaveholders, some Catholic slaveholders of southeastern Louisiana vigorously concerned themselves with the religious lives of their slaves. The Zeringues were quite zealous in their effort to convert their slaves to Catholicism. There is evidence to suggest that the Zeringues, like some of their other Catholic slaveholding counterparts, looked favorably on slaves who conformed to their religious norms. In 1842, the Widow Zeringue (Camille's mother) gave her permission for Eugene, the son of a female slave named Eulalie, to be baptized.[32]

This was significant, because throughout the South many slave owners sought to diminish the importance of religion in the lives of their slaves. Slaveholders in Louisiana and elsewhere often forbade religion and faith practices among their slaves. Nothing could have been further from the truth on the Zeringue plantation. In fact, the Zeringues' religious enthusiasm prompted regular trips to church. The family took a boat across the Mississippi River to attend mass, taking along as many slaves as the boat would hold. It is said that it was quite a sight to behold the great planter and his wife, followed by their children and dozens of slaves, making their way into the church.[33]

In addition to their efforts to Christianize their slaves, the Zeringues invited Sister Marie Jeanne Aliquot, a Roman Catholic nun, to live on their plantation. Sister Aliquot's primary duty was to instruct the slaves in various skills and, most important, in the catechism of the Catholic Church. Again, in this practice the Zeringue family broke from the norms of the traditional slaveholding culture. It was common throughout the South for the master to forbid most forms of schooling among slaves. Reading was often especially forbidden. But the Zeringue family encouraged learning among its slaves.

Why the Zeringues differed so remarkably from their contemporaries on issues of religion and schooling among their slaves is difficult to ascertain. Certainly their position as Catholics played a role, but a deeper meaning may be inferred. The Zeringues, especially Camille, were an independent family who, while conforming to the culture of the day in many respects, were equally happy to disregard societal mores and customs for those they felt more appropriate. This gives insight into the general class and place this family was in at the time. Most minor plantation families climbing the social ladder in the rigid Louisiana aristocracy of the planter elite would have felt it necessary to model their behavior precisely on that of the majority of their more successful and prominent neighbors. The Zeringues, however, were at the pinnacle of this society. Secure now in a place where their behavior was much less controlled by the desire to break into the upper echelon, it is quite likely the family even acted as antebellum trendsetters. As Sister Aliqout was a frequent visitor to the Zeringue plantation, she soon became a regular fixture at many of the larger estates along the Mississippi, visiting Mrs. Waggaman, for example, on the Waggaman plantation to the west to bring her unique ministry there.

The position of Sister Aliquot must have been an unusual one. She was a nun, a religious sister, in a position of religious authority respected greatly by Roman Catholics but at the same time ministered to those who were considered to be among the lowest on the socioeconomic scale, individuals who were held as property. She was also a woman in a time when women were marginalized by a male-dominated society. How Sister Aliquot successfully juggled these paradoxical identities we may never know, but, it is certain that she transcended her position in life through her active role as a religious leader. Aliquot, among other things, helped Henriette Delille, a free woman of color, to found the Sisters of the Holy Family, a religious order of African-American women that is still very active today. Aside from simply providing education for the slaves, Sister Aliquot became a religious authority and leader for the entire community along the Great River Road, ministering to many of the great plantation families of the region.

Sister Aliquot's work on the sugar plantations along the river was unique compared to the rest of the plantation South. Though women did hold positions of religious authority in other parts of the South, they were usually quite limited. Sister Aliquot, however, was a female religious authority looked upon with reverence by the entire local community, including the elite planters and their families. She was an incredibly mobile and independent woman of her time, crossing the Mississippi River and going from plantation to plantation along the river's banks. It is clear that Sister Aliquot used her unusual position to her advantage, to transcend, at least partially, her "inferior" position in society and to aid those in most need of her assistance, those whom society viewed only as the property of their masters. This situation was a direct result of the religious background of the area; the Roman Catholic planters identified Sister Aliquot as a religious leader above all else.

In a letter to Father Stephen Rousselon, Sister Aliquot stated that when she left the Zeringue plantation, the eldest daughter gave money, for which she was quite proud. Growing up in their deeply spiritual household and under the devoutly religious influence of their beloved Sister Aliquot, Zeringue's children became very practical, spiritual people. Zeringue's daughters followed in the footsteps of Sister Aliquot by devoting their lives to God and joining a religious order.[34]

The Plantation
and the Civil War

The American people and the Government at Washington may refuse to
recognize it for a time but the inexorable logic of events will force it
upon them in the end; that the war now being waged in this land is a
war for and against slavery.

—FREDRICK DOUGLASS

America has no north, no south, no east, no west. The sun rises over
the hills and sets over the mountains, the compass just points up and
down, and we can laugh now at the absurd notion of there being a
north and a south. We are one and undivided.

—SAM WATKINS, 1ST TENNESSEE REGIMENT

The Zeringues led a life of great splendor and privilege provided partly by the
forced labor of enslaved individuals, and, in 1861, when Louisiana withdrew
from the union, the family took up the cause for southern sovereignty. As a
business owner who relied on slavery for the prosperity of his plantation,
Zeringue willingly helped finance the Confederate cause. During this time,
many planters made large personal financial contributions toward the war.
Planters like Zeringue believed strongly in southern independence, and sentiment was strong that the South would prevail in any military conflicts with
northern states. So strong was this belief that planters invested much. They
rallied troops, and the planter-led police juries allocated funds for military
purposes. An elite cavalry unit known as the Jefferson Rangers received funding of one thousand dollars from the Jefferson Parish Police Jury.[1]

In the early days of Louisiana's secession, the war was an abstract, faraway event to be read about in newspapers and talked about in town.

A pervasive spirit of southern pride thrived through local communities and in households, and tense excitement filled the air. Although credit was tightened and Zeringue and his fellow planters felt the economic woes of war, routine continued on most plantations as it had for decades; planting, harvesting, and grinding took place as if nothing of any consequence was occurring beyond the plantation, producing a bumper sugar crop in 1861.

Other things remained the same as well. Even on the eve of invasion, planters and their families continued to enjoy lavish balls and social events as young men went to war. In her journal, Eliza Francis Andrews commented on this seemingly contradictory situation: "It may seem strange to the modern reader that in the midst of such tremendous happenings we could find it in our hearts to go about the common business of life; to laugh and dance and be merry in spite of the crumbling of the social fabric about us. But so it has always been; so it was 'in the days of Noe,' and so, we are told, will it be 'in the end of the world.' Youth will have its innings, and never was social life in the old South more full of charm than when tottering to its fall."[2]

Most planters felt optimistic about the sugar market during secession, never fully realizing that war would have a major effect on their ability to sell and transport their crop. It wasn't until the Union Navy seized the Gulf of Mexico and blocked the mouth of the Mississippi that planters realized their problems. With the mouth of the river impenetrable, there was virtually no way for planters to get their large crops to market. The price of sugar plummeted, whereas the cost of food and other necessities increased. Louisiana sugar planters' "white gold" was quickly turning to worthless "white dust." Camille Zeringue, along with sugar planters throughout the state, now felt the economic hardships of war, making it difficult, if not impossible, to feed and clothe their own slaves.[3]

Rallying to the battle cry of the Confederacy, many sons of sugar planters made their way to war. No different was the situation in the Zeringue family, and, on October 12, 1863, Zeringue's son, Jene Fortuné Zeringue, enlisted as a private at Mobile, Alabama.[4] He joined Company F (Orleans Guards) of the 30th Louisiana Infantry, commanded by Louis Fortin. The 30th Infantry, also known as Sumter Regiment, was originally organized into state service at New Orleans in December 1861. On March 1, 1862, this regiment was transferred into Confederate service for ninety days. Part of the regiment surrendered at New Orleans on April 26, 1862, and the group was subsequently reorganized at Camp Moore to the north in Tangipahoa Parish the following month.[5] Camille's other sons, Michael and Edmond, also joined their brother in battle.

As many sugar planters and even more of their sons joined Confederate forces, their plantations were left to become the sites of battles and skirmishes. With their husbands and sons gone, ladies of the plantations were left to fend for themselves and their homes and often watched helplessly as battles and conflicts commenced in their fields. Evidence shows that Confederate soldiers were stationed on the Zeringue Plantation. The Confederates built fortifications and a strong military line where troops were stationed on one side of the Barataria and Lafourche Canal on Zeringue's plantation. Other battles commenced around the estate, and combat likely took place in the heart or on the outskirts of the plantation itself (fig. 8).[6]

These soldiers would have probably made their way to the region via the New Orleans, Opelousas, and Great Western Railroad line. Zeringue had granted the right-of-way through his plantation to the railroad on October 14, 1852, with the condition that no station be placed on any of his property. The line made a stop, known then as Jefferson's Station, near the plantation. When riding through the area, one Southerner wrote, "along the route, it is cane, cane, hardly anything else than cane. For acres and acres, and even miles together, on both sides of the road, and sometimes as far as the eye can reach, the green expanse of high vigorous cane stretched away in rich profusion."[7]

As they reached the plantation, Confederate troops disembarked from the railcars and set up camp along the canal. The Zeringues probably welcomed such troops and willingly provided them with a variety of necessities, including the labor of their slaves. According to Mildred Stehle Harris, one of the twentieth-century occupants of the mansion, when she and her family first moved into the house in 1919, they met a man named Celest who claimed to have been a slave owned by the Zeringues. Celest told the family that during the Civil War he accompanied troops (who were stationed on or near the plantation) and played the drums—further evidence that the Zeringue Plantation was a point of war activity.[8]

It was not uncommon for Confederate troops to be stationed on sugar plantations, and, when they were, the officers and soldiers enjoyed the generous hospitality of the planter and his family. Often the daughters were quite lonely and distraught, as their male suitors, the sons of other planters, marched off to war. To fill this void in their social lives, these young ladies

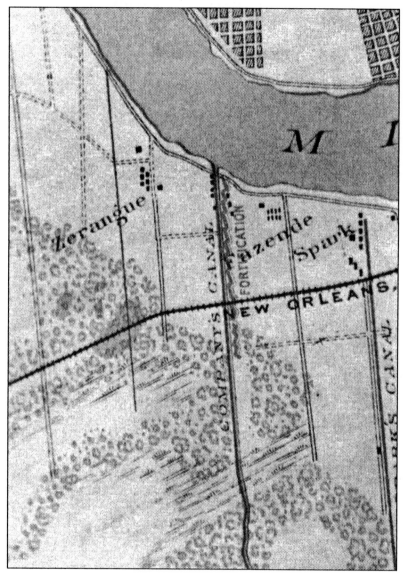

Fig. 8. This 1863 map of the Zeringue and neighboring plantations shows the area with the Confederate fortification marked on the eastern side of the "Company's Canal." Map courtesy of Daniel P. Alario Sr., Westwego, Louisiana.

often busied themselves by visiting the encampments, bringing food, liquor, and sweets for the men. It was nearly impossible to visit the encampments without seeing young southern belles chatting and flirting with the soldiers or mending their wounds. The presence of young Confederate officers restored the social life of the surrounding plantations, especially that of the planters' daughters. Often planters invited the officers to dine in their mansions, which "invariably put the girls into a dither." It was not uncommon, after dinner, for the girls to take the officers on a late night tour of the sugarhouse, especially during the grinding season when the slaves were busy producing sugar. Interestingly, it was not as uncommon as would be imagined for southern planters to invite Union officers to dine in their mansions—an invitation not wholly motivated by hospitality, as planters by necessity advanced friendships with Yankees for the favors they so desperately needed.[9]

Soon, the pleasantries of socializing were distant memories as the war itself was no longer a vague idea; it had become a blatant reality as violence descended on the Zeringue plantation. The union forces marched through the vast cane fields toward the Confederate encampment along the canal. Fighting in the sugarcane fields of southeastern Louisiana differed vastly from combat elsewhere. The rugged terrain of the fields made for a difficult time regardless of what side one fought for.[10] It was not uncommon for the women on the plantation to witness the violent and unsightly acts of battle. One of Zeringue's daughters said that as Federals invaded the plantation and overtook the Confederate troops, she and her sisters and mother fled to New Orleans to seek refuge.[11]

Unfortunately, New Orleans was a safe haven for the Zeringue women for only a short time. On April 25, 1862, Confederate soldiers fought Union soldiers seeking to seize the city. The Union considered New Orleans not only an international city of monumental importance but, also, the largest city of the Confederacy. The battle ended on May 1, 1862, with the Union striking another victory. Under Union occupation, officials organized new courts and established a military government at New Orleans. With the invasion of the area by Union troops came the abrupt realities of war. The culture and way of life the planters and their families had always known was dying. For the sugar planters, the cheerful, light days of faraway war were ended. "No longer did they relax on their verandas, drinking mint juleps and discoursing on the ineffectiveness of naval blockade and the impending collapse of the Northern economy. Gone were the dangerous illusions concerning the pre-eminence of King Cotton and the invincibility of Southern arms. The Mississippi—friend and benefactor in time of peace—had betrayed them in time of war and had borne the invader into their midst. Mansions stood empty and pillaged, with idle sugar houses falling rapidly into ruin. The fields were littered with rotten cane. Desolation overshadowed the plantation country."[12]

While the Union held New Orleans under siege, the people within the city, including Zeringue's wife and daughters, felt the hardships of their limited communication, transportation, and trade. Food became scarce, so Union officials opened the blockaded New Orleans, Opelousas, and Great Western railroad lines in order to transport food into the city.

Meanwhile, rebel troops on the west bank concocted their own plans. On May 26, 1862, the St. Martin Rangers captured a train at Bayou Boeuf. They raced down the railroad line, as far as Jefferson's Station near the Zeringue Plantation. The troops disembarked the train near the estate and dismantled the tracks in an act of sabotage aimed at the Union cause. They took the rails and burned bridges along their way to the southwest to Brashear City (now Morgan City).[13] Union forces quickly repaired the damages, further expressing their control of the region.

Union domination was only further substantiated when on January 1, 1863, President Abraham Lincoln presented his Emancipation Proclamation, which ordered all slaves to be set free and sought the abolishment of slavery in America. The following year, a convention elected from the Union element of the state presented a new constitution that required the immediate and unconditional release of all slaves in Louisiana.

By 1864, Louisiana's sugar industry was all but devastated. Few planters sought to make a crop that year. Many planned to grind their seed cane, abandoning the sugar culture entirely, although Zeringue had plans to rebuild his business and try again. Greatly disturbed by the decline of the sugar industry and by some of the planters' plan to mill their seed cane, General Nathaniel P. Banks ordered all sugar planters to reserve one fourth of their 1864 crop for seed. This order further decreased the amount of sugar produced. Cuban sugar had to be shipped in to meet the demand in New Orleans. Many sugar planters turned to other crops, especially cotton and rice, as the processes involved in producing these crops were less labor intensive and required less capital. Vegetable cultivation also increased on sugar plantations.[14]

The availability of needed capital had become a real problem for Louisiana sugar planters. Sugar planters operated on credit, which was advanced by factors. Problems arose as early as 1862, when Federal troops invaded some sugar areas, demoralizing the work ethics of the slaves and confiscating the plantation livestock. Unable to produce an adequate crop, the planters could not pay debts, ruining factors and the banks that supported them. By 1864, fewer than 2 percent of the five hundred or so antebellum factors were still in business, and most of the South's banks had gone under as well.[15]

Compounding the problems faced by sugar planters was the dissolution of slavery, the foundation of their great labor force. The end of the "particular institution" was a reality-shattering experience for both blacks and whites. Many former slaves were unprepared to leave the plantation, the only homes many had ever known; others celebrated their new freedom. It is said that after they gained their freedom none of the Zeringue slaves wished to leave their plantation home, and some are reported to have remained on or near the plantation for the rest of their lives.

Camille Zeringue, along with many of his fellow planters, suffered great financial losses during the war. In 1866, authorities seized and auctioned off much of his property, including "cane knives (used in harvesting sugar cane), a cotton gin and cotton press, a corn mill, a mowing machine, 32 stacks of rice in sacks, 200 barrels of threshed rice in sacks, a saw mill, hogs, cows, a bull, mules, oxen, chickens and pigeons, horses, plows, carts and tools."[16] The great variety of machinery and animals auctioned gives a glimpse into the variety of crops and livestock that Zeringue raised and harvested at his plantation. In addition to these losses, many planters also found that much of their livestock, including horses and mules, was taken into the custody of the Union forces. The impressment of livestock, including horses and mules, by Union forces was a blow that nearly all planters felt. Planters, like Zeringue, also found northern soldiers were not hospitable guests on their estates. Rowdy young Union men were anxious to seek revenge upon wealthy southern planters and caused incalculable damage on plantations across the South. Looting and vandalism were common.[17]

But, for all the physical losses suffered by planters, none were as great as the personal losses they endured. At least one of Zeringue's sons was killed in the war somewhere near Atlanta. Zeringue's daughters recount hearing the news of their brother's death while still in exile in New Orleans. Adding to the family's heartbreak was the possibility that another of Zeringue's sons had died and a third son, Jean Fortuné, returning home from the war badly injured and crippled.[18]

On March 2, 1867, General Philip Henry Sheridan took control of Louisiana as it became part of the Fifth Military District. As officials ratified the Fourteenth Amendment to the United States Constitution, Louisiana adopted a new constitution of its own, one that enfranchised blacks. Military occupation in the state came to an end in July of the same year.

The war had ravaged Zeringue and other planters throughout the South. Reconstruction brought with it a new beginning for these planters, who started over humbly, with their businesses and their lives. One of the major problems still faced by Zeringue and his fellow planters was a shortage of labor. No longer were these businessmen able to rely on the institution of slavery to provide the large amount of physical labor needed to run a plantation.

Interestingly, many of the emancipated slaves continued to live on Zeringue's plantation, but no longer were these laborers the property of their master. They were now employees, a fact that would change the dynamics of plantation life and society. Research shows that in the sugar parishes, freed blacks often continued working on the plantation, cultivating cane and producing sugar. They actively and wholeheartedly negotiated for fair pay and better working conditions in exchange for their labor, a commodity that was crucial on the plantation. Often these negotiations led to strife, but in some instances they functioned to create a mutually beneficial working environment. Regardless, the new labor system obliterated the economic system associated with sugar planting before the war. This often led to devastation for former slave-owning sugar planters. Zeringue's daughters noted that it was the emancipation of the slaves that ultimately led to the plantation's ruin, and they were probably correct in this observation.[19]

Soon after their emancipation, a number of the former slaves built a church at the plantation's lower boundary near the canal and river. This congregation, known as Little True Vine, was said to have been inspired by the Rev. Thomas Peterson of the Zion Travelers First Baptist Church across the river in the Carrollton section of Jefferson Parish. The Zeringue slaves knew him before their emancipation, and he probably played an important role in the establishment of their congregation in the slave cabins long before they built their church. A little community of former slaves, known as "Red Bean Row," soon developed around the church.

In many ways, the formation of this church and congregation may be seen as a form of passive resistance on the part of many of the former slaves. Even before their emancipation, the slaves were worshiping in the slave cabins and actively developing a Protestant congregation. The Zeringues were devout Catholics, and as noted earlier, they aggressively tried to convert their slaves. By rejecting their master's deeply held religion, the slaves were asserting that they were individuals with the rights and ability to choose their own personal beliefs, faith, and religious practices. The establishment of this congregation, outside the reach of their master's influence, also allowed the slaves to bond in a cohesive social group, permitting support and organized resistance efforts.

After the Civil War, three of Zeringue's daughters, like the former slaves, began seeking lives of their own away from their plantation home. Their short biographies provide much insight into the life of the family and also into the religious careers of these three pious women. Following in the footsteps of their beloved friend Sister Aliquot, Marie Ann Lise, Marie Celeste, and Camille all joined the Society of the Sacred Heart. Within the society, the women devoted themselves to God, living simple lives of servitude as "brides of Christ."

Camille was the first to enter the order, in 1865 at age thirty-one. She was brought to the convent at St. Michael's, Louisiana, by her brother, Jean Fortuné, who had been injured in the war. At St. Michael's, Camille was known among her fellow nuns for her generosity and charity; she was also known for her lively playfulness and outgoing personality. Certainly not the stereotypical stern religious sister, Camille delighted the other nuns with her lightheartedness and joviality. She took the habit of the order on March 9, 1866, along with four other women, all of whom were above the usual age. These five women became known throughout the society as "The Famous Five" because of their fervor, generosity, and spiritual devotion. Camille made her first vows in the society on March 20, 1868.[20]

The fact that Camille and her sisters joined a religious order gives much insight into the Zeringue family. Obviously the Zeringues were deeply religious people. Camille Zeringue, the planter, had priests stay at his plantation, built an altar for mass, and regularly brought slaves across the river for mass. In addition, a nun lived from time to time on the plantation, inspiring Zeringue's daughters to become nuns.

One might ask how such obviously religious people could reconcile owing slaves with their devout Christianity. Paternalistic sentiment was pervasive in that time and place, and the Zeringues did not see slavery as an evil thing. The Zeringue daughters even expressed how much they were helping those whom they enslaved, displaying a culturally ingrained mindset that was certainly more palatable than the reality of the situation.

Sister Camille's early religious life would only foreshadow her later accomplishments. Her entire religious life would, fascinatingly, be mystically intertwined with John Berchmans, a young Belgium man who had lived in the seventeenth century. Berchmans died an untimely death while studying to be a Jesuit priest. During Camille's first year as a novice in the Society of the Sacred Heart, the miraculous healing of a woman named Mary Wilson was attributed to Berchmans. Camille had been charged with decorating the altar in this woman's room (where she was dying) and had frequent conversations with her. Wilson's spontaneous healing intrigued Camille greatly. Whereas some of the novices became terrified by the strange healing, Camille joyfully exclaimed, "But we have asked for a miracle and we have obtained it, that I am sure of!" She immersed herself in studying the pious young man's life. Over the years, she grew quite close to the memory of this young man, calling him simply, "Brother John." Camille was later called to submit a deposition before a grand ecclesiastical commission, which was investigating Berchmans's cause for canonization. It is said that after Berchmans's 1888 canonization Camille often threatened him, saying that if he didn't answer her prayers promptly, she would no longer call him "St. John Berchmans." Her father's steadfastness and even obstinacy could certainly be seen in her personality.

In the meantime, Camille was joined in the society by her two sisters. Marie Ann Lise entered the society's convent at Grand Coteau on October 2, 1882, and Marie Celeste entered the convent at St. Michael's on March 17, 1893. Like her sisters, Marie Ann Lise first came into contact with the Sisters of the Sacred Heart at St. Michael's when she was sent there as a child to prepare for her first communion. When she arrived, the convent was a "tower of Babel" with novices speaking French, Spanish, English, and possibly other languages. The Superior of the novitiate house, Mother Metzler, spoke many languages and succeeded in maintaining some level of order in the house. Throughout her life, Marie Ann Lise was recognized for her talent with words.

Whenever guests visited the house, she had charming words of welcome that made them feel at home. She took her first vows on December 8, 1884. She then traveled to Paris, where her profession in the Society was later made.

Marie Ann Lise returned to Louisiana and was devoted to the care of the sick at Grand Coteau. She gallantly attended to all those who sought care, even going into quarantine with a child who was suffering from scarlet fever. She also was distinguished for her steadfastness toward the vow of poverty, even fishing little scraps of cloth or paper from the trash to use again to repair a sister's habit or for writing a letter.

It is said that Marie Celeste wished to follow her two sisters earlier in her life, but family duty prevented it. She remained on the plantation to aid and care for their mother. It seems that after taking her vows, it was Celeste's obligation, or perhaps her wish, to seek solitude away from the convent. Hearing this, Camille grew very upset, not wanting her younger sister to travel alone. She immediately consulted in prayer with her beloved "Brother John." He did not seem to answer her prayers immediately, and Camille threatened him ardently. She said that if he didn't listen to her she would never again call him "St. John." Miraculously, after this stern threat, Camille's prayers were answered, and a traveling companion was found for Celeste. Upon return from her sabbatical, Celeste spent the rest of her days caring for the sick at St. Michael's.

Throughout their careers, the three sisters continued their childhood hobby of artificial flower making. They prided themselves on the crowns they made for students receiving their first communion and on the decorations they created for the annual Feast of the Superiors. It was said that the baskets of flowers and plumes were an extraordinary addition to these festive occasions. The sisters also crafted lifelike birds and squirrels from a variety of natural materials.

The three Zeringue sisters worked caring for the sick, but Sister Camille earned the position of "Mistress of Health" in the convent, overseeing all health care. Despite her love for this work, her real calling was to work with children. When two small, orphaned children were brought to the convent, Camille immediately rejoiced in their care. The younger child, who was two, clung especially to her.

Camille's devotion and skill earned her the position of Superior at the society's convent in New Orleans. There she practiced her faith through practical examples. One day when one of the younger sisters had left a piece of bread on the breakfast table, Mother Camille put it on a saucer and carried it throughout the convent. By the time it was growing mold, the other sisters began to inquire why their superior carried around this moldy bread. Camille responded that it was to teach the young sisters a lesson about the evils of wastefulness. She further added that she intended to eat the moldy bread at dinner. She ignored protests from the sisters and consumed the bread at dinner that night.

In another instance, she sought to teach another young sister the importance of orderliness. During morning prayers, Camille touched the girl's shoulder and beckoned her to follow. She led her through the convent into the girl's bedroom or "cell." The room was littered with all sorts of things. Camille looked sternly at the young nun and asked, "Is this the alcove of a virgin of the Lord?" The young sister immediately cleaned the room.

Camille left her position as Superior in New Orleans and returned to St. Michael's for a short while before leaving the country to serve in San Luis Potosi, Mexico. While there, she served as Mistress of Health. On one occasion, Camille was left in charge of the house when the Superior was absent. During this time, the Mistress of the Poor contracted a vile contagious illness after contact with an infected child. Quarantine was necessary. A small house was rented across the street from the convent, and Camille quarantined herself with the sick nun. From the window of the little house, she gave a nightly report to the sisters in the convent. Her report was always quite grave, and, as nights passed, it grew even worse. After twelve days, the Mistress of the Poor died. Soon after, Camille herself began to grow ill, having contracted this grave illness from her patient. She prayed passionately and, within a short time, was miraculously healed. Even though she never learned the language, Camille grew to love Mexico and the Mexican people, but her service there was not to be permanent.

In 1888, she returned to Grand Coteau. She served there again as Mistress of Health and later opened a school for black children. She loved working with the children, whom she often called her "little chocolate pralines." She placed iron crosses, representing the Stations of the Cross, in the cemetery where she took the children often to teach them this devotion. She also taught the children how to sew and make vestments. Interestingly, twenty of the girls Camille taught later joined the Sisters of the Holy

Family, the order of black nuns with which Sister Aliquot (the beloved nun who resided on the Zeringue plantation) was associated. This was fitting, as it was Sister Aliquot who first inspired the Zeringue girls to become nuns. When once asked what the secret to her devotion was, Sister Camille responded, "Oh well, when I enter the chapel, I leave all my distractions at the door like a traveler who attaches his horse to the post."

As the years passed, the world outside began to change, and the Zeringue sisters began to feel the burdens that came with age. Now automobiles, electricity, and telephones were all the rage; but it is said that Camille cared nothing for these new inventions, longing instead for the days of yesteryear. Camille had once said, "In our society it is thus, today on the chandelier, tomorrow in the farm yard." Certainly, by this time she had witnessed her father's tragic decline from powerful planter ravaged by the Civil War to a poor farmer struggling to reclaim his life after the resolution of the Union.

Camille was right in her observation of the swift decline one finds in life, as the joy found in her constant service to others would be no more. With age, deafness besieged both Camille and Marie Ann Lise, who often kept each other company. The younger sisters of the order found humor in this pair, as the two old women would often berate and criticize one another, but because of their deafness, neither could hear what the other said. Unable to continue her duties as a teacher and health-care provider, Camille spent her days in prayer, praying for various petitions of the house. These prayers are said to have often obtained immediate and miraculous effects. In 1920, she prayed for a nun who had injured her leg in an accident that had taken the lives of two other nuns. Camille prayed and rubbed the woman's leg, and, soon after, it was healed.

Marie Celeste had some sort of attack at St. Michael's and, over the weeks, grew quite ill. As she was dying, the convent received a visit from the Mother Vicar, who took time to pray with her during her last days. She said, summing up her life's work simply, "I do always the little I can do." Marie Celeste died on February 1, 1923.

A few months later, at age eighty-eight, Camille Zeringue followed her sister in death. She grew gravely ill and received the last sacrament. A special candle, which had been brought from Rome from the canonization ceremonies of St. John Berchmans, burned near her bed. In the end, she called out to her beloved "Brother John," and shortly before breathing her lasts breath, she looked up to Heaven and asked St. Peter to "put a little oil on the gates of Heaven so that they might open easily for this poor sinner." She died on August 12, 1923, a little more than a month before her golden jubilee of her formal profession into the Society of the Sacred Heart.

Marie Ann Lise lived a few more years in Grand Coteau. In her old age, she could also be found in the chapel bent over kneeling for hours in prayer, often falling with nothing to support herself. It is said that during her last days she often suffered in silence but voiced her desire to meet her spouse (Christ). Finally, on March 28, 1928, she died at the exact moment the sisters of the house completed their evening prayers.

Although the stories of the lives of these fascinating women are certainly interesting unto themselves, they also reveal much about the Zeringues and life on their plantation. It was clear that each of the Zeringue sisters was steadfast and devout. They were very practical people who showed resourcefulness and frugality—all qualities that would have been essential, even for the planter's daughters, on a self-sufficient antebellum plantation.

The women's devotion not only speaks volumes to the Zeringue family's own faith and the importance of organized religion in their lives but also gives insight into the family's underlying determination and strength, qualities that allowed the family to survive, although battered, through the Civil War. It is clear that just as their religious lives were nurtured in their convents, the traits and value systems held throughout their lives were greatly influenced and cultivated in their plantation home.

CHAPTER SIX

The Railroad Ruckus

Shall the railroads govern the country, or shall the people govern the
railroads? Shall the interest of railroad kings be chiefly regarded, or shall
the interest of the people be paramount?

—PRESIDENT RUTHERFORD B. HAYES

On October 14, 1852, Camille Zeringue granted a right-of-way through
his plantation to the New Orleans, Opelousas, and Great Western Railroad
with the condition that no station be placed on any of his property. The
construction of the railroad lines across the enormous fields commenced,
and soon steam engines could be regularly seen charging through the sugarcane. These same lines, which later carried troops to their canal-side
camp and played a minor role in the Civil War, caused Zeringue a great
deal of frustration in his last days.

The war left the Louisiana sugar industry badly bruised. The Zeringues,
like other area planters, felt this economic blow, having much of their plantation equipment and property seized and suffering financial losses from
their funding of the war. In addition, the capital in the form of credit that
planters like Zeringue had relied on throughout their careers was no longer
readily available. To make matters worse, wartime inflation ensured costly
prices of replacement equipment, supplies, and virtually all the physical necessities of the plantation. In order to amend his disastrous financial situation,
Zeringue mortgaged his plantation. Despite his fiscal hardships, he was one
of the lucky ones, as he was fortunate enough to keep his estate. Many of those
with a similar fortune found that their sugarhouses and equipment had been
damaged or destroyed by Union vandals or by years of disuse. The great
sugar plantations along the river were in terrible condition—their levees

broken, ditches overgrown, fields untended, buildings in disrepair, and animals gone.[1] Further adding to the planters' woes, the labor force was reduced, and those former slaves who remained on the plantation were no longer the property of their masters and were unwilling to be treated as slaves.

Camille Zeringue and his fellow planter elite were no longer the masters of social, political, and economic life. Many of the most successful planters found themselves in ruin after the war. The old social order that maintained planters in the highest class of their community was gone forever. Planters were reduced to poor farmers often without labor to farm their lands.

Zeringue was also personally disappointed to find that the ambitious canal, whose construction he had spearheaded, was faced with competition from another transportation source. After the war, the railroads began to dominate the area, and they slowly became competition for the Company Canal. Fewer steamboats made their way down the canal, as more railway cars passed through the plantation's fields. Even though Zeringue had given railroad officials the right-of-way through his property, after the war ended, they demanded more.

Railroad officials began to search for an acceptable place to build a railroad terminal. After much searching, the Ames Group (which controlled the railroad at the time) spotted the great Zeringue Plantation. Noted railroad engineer G. W. R. Bayley[2] stated that the Zeringue plantation was "the first place on the right bank of the river, above the terminus of Morgan's Louisiana and Texas Railroad—8 miles down the river—where the river bank is stationary or where there is no accretion or caving and where wharves for railway use will be comparatively permanent." He further added that this site was "an important requisite for a railway terminus on the Mississippi River."[3]

The Ames Group purchased the right-of-way across the Zeringue plantation and soon reorganized into the Texas and Pacific Railroad. After continuing to eye the land surrounding their right-of-way, railroad officials approached Camille Zeringue. They wanted to build a terminal between the master house and the Company Canal. The railroad wanted all 183 acres separating the house from the canal. At this time, the entire plantation was appraised at $100,000, and the 183 acres lying between the canal and the house was appraised at $37,500. The railroad was willing to pay. Zeringue did not accept the railroad's offer, realizing the headaches a railroad terminal in his own yard and gardens would cause. The railroad company not only wanted to construct a terminal, it also wanted to build terminal wharves approximately 1,400 feet away from Zeringue's mansion and 25 feet away from the overseer's house. A bridge spanning the Mississippi River did not exist at the time, so railroad cars would have to be transported across the river by ferryboats. A large landing and wharves were required in order to take cars from the ferry and reposition them on tracks.[4]

The Louisiana legislature, pressured by the railroad officials, had given railroad companies the power to expropriate land in any way they saw fit. This arrangement was supposed to hasten the completion of railway lines; it also gave the railroads the right to take private property from citizens all across the state. After Zeringue's refusal to sell, the railroad quickly filed suit to seize the property. The trial occurred in May 1870. At this time, L. C. Lebreton operated the plantation on behalf of Zeringue, who was now elderly. Lebreton testified that a railway terminal would ruin the house and gardens as well as destroy the tranquility and peace of the entire plantation. He also noted the problems that the various workmen would cause to the plantation. C. S. Fazende, Zeringue's neighbor and the superintendent of the Barataria and Lafourche Canal, also testified. He brought up examples of how planters were unable to grow crops next to the terminals of the reorganized Great Western and the New Orleans Opelousas railroads, because of the many people who used the railway terminal. They testified that these people would walk through the fields, plunder and pillage, and eventually ruin the crops.[5]

William Gordon also testified on Zeringue's behalf. He explained to the court that he had surveyed the plantation and believed the railroad could find much more suitable land for the terminal. He told the court that Zeringue's land was low and not well drained. He also said that he had examined the soil and found it to be very sandy. He explained that he found a "salty mixture" throughout the soil.[6]

Camille Zeringue, eighty years old, also testified in court. He made it clear that if a railroad terminal was to be built on his property, he wanted no less than $200,000 for the land. His point was that by taking the land, the railroad would eventually destroy the entire plantation, and if they wanted any piece of the property, it would only be proper that they buy the entire plantation from him. Zeringue told the court the story of a Mr. Woodruff, who offered him $175,000 for the plantation. Zeringue refused this offer, and then Woodruff offered Zeringue a lesser price. "I told him it was ridiculous to think that I would take less when I refused the greater price," he said. Later, Zeringue told the court, "I will not sell for less than $200,000." Zeringue's notorious hot temper and stubborn ways were sure to have shown themselves throughout this most difficult time. He believed in his rights as a property owner and was quite disgusted by the railroad company's attempt to seize his beloved plantation. Zeringue was also surely upset at the cultural and societal changes that the war had wrought. No longer did the planter elite wield near limitless power within their communities and in the courts. Times had changed, and industry was thought to be the savior of the South.[7]

The trial continued as Mr. P. Boisblanc testified for the railroad, assessing Zeringue's entire plantation at $150,000. Boisblanc also argued that by taking the land that rests between the canal and mansion, the railroad would be leaving Zeringue with the best part of the property. Zeringue vehemently disagreed. He felt as though a railroad terminal would limit his interaction with the Mississippi River, the most crucial route of transportation and communication for plantation communities. "I would be cut off from all intercourse with the River." Zeringue said.[8]

The arguments against the railroad terminals were all in vain, as courts allowed the railroad to purchase the property between the house and canal. The railroad quickly began construction on the site of the plantation. The railroad called the area Westwego, a name that had never been used before and, for many decades, was to remain a term used solely to refer to the railroad docks and yard.

The verdict in this case speaks clearly to the state of Zeringue and his fellow planter elite. In previous legal cases (*Camille Zeringue vs. Holmes and Parsons*, and *Jonas Pickles vs. Camille Zeringue*), Zeringue's supremacy as a member of the ruling class was without question. The verdict in the railroad case not only gives insight into the political dominance of the railroad in the postwar South but also demonstrates the greatly declining social, political, and economic status of Zeringue and his fellow plantation owners. No longer were these once wealthy men masters over man and society; instead they were reduced to average citizens. Zeringue was more than aware of this verdict's ultimate meaning for his status in the new social order.

Zeringue was an old man, and the culture and society he knew and flourished in had crumbled around him. The bitter battle with railroad officials had also upset him a great deal. His last days were spent watching railroad workmen construct huge industrial structures on the peaceful green area between his mansion and the canal he had built. Zeringue died on January 6, 1872, at his plantation mansion at age eighty-two. An obituary published in the *Daily Picayune* on the day after his death reported that the funeral would take place on Sunday, January 7, 1872, at St. Mary's Church. The funeral would be followed by a march to St. Louis Cemetery.[9]

Zeringue had lived a long, successful life, serving his community as a local leader, an exemplary statesman, and a profitable businessman. He was a passionate father and planter who had the unique experience of living in two different worlds. He was born into an antebellum South ruled by the planter elite and died in a post-Civil War Louisiana very different from the reality he had previously known. His survivors included his widow and several children. Zeringue's widow and son, Jean Fortuné, were made co-administrators of the estate. On January 25, 1872, Jean Fortuné Zeringue became the "true and lawful attorney of all community and succession property." Camille Zeringue's will, dated ten days prior to his death, asked that his land not be divided during the lifetime of his widow.[10]

Sadly, the family did not abide by Zeringue's wishes. Jean Fortuné ran the plantation, surviving by selling pieces of the property to railroads and mortgaging others. Most of the land sold was soon developed, as the railroad and other local industries grew. With the great economic effects of the war still being felt strongly throughout the South, the success previously achieved by the plantation in antebellum days was not to be seen again. The situation was no different for Jean Fortuné, who was unable to amass the substantial profits his father had.[11]

When the mortgage Camille Zeringue had made with the Consolidated Planters Association was due, Jean Fortuné mortgaged $15,000 worth of stock to the Citizens Bank of Louisiana. Soon this mortgage was also due, and Jean Fortuné could not pay it. The Zeringues lost the plantation through foreclosure. The Citizens Bank of Louisiana acquired the remainder of the Zeringue plantation by sheriff's deed from the widow and heirs of Camille Zeringue on November 16, 1891.[12]

The railroad filed for bankruptcy. A group of investors from St. Louis purchased it and, in September 1882, opened railroad lines from New Orleans to Shreveport. This company later became the Missouri Pacific Railroad. At this time, surveyors described the Zeringue plantation as containing thirty-four arpents of land.

On March 7, 1892, Pablo Sala purchased the plantation from the Citizens Bank of Louisiana. Sala was instrumental in establishing a permanent settlement near the plantation, an area that came to be known as "Salaville," and for the short time he owned the Zeringue plantation he succeeded in transforming it into a highly successful resort.[13]

The next month, on April 17, 1892, the widow Zeringue died at age eighty-three. An obituary printed in the *Daily Picayune* invited "friends and acquaintances of the Zeringue, Roman, Lombard, and LeBreton families" to a funeral on the following evening held at her New Orleans residence at 237 Bayou Road.[14]

Although Camille Zeringue did not live to see his beloved plantation taken from his family, his widow did. She died with her family's substantial plantation and the entire social order and wealth she once knew now gone forever. Her death ended the final chapter of the Zeringues at Seven Oaks. Like a symbol of the old South itself, Madeline exited this world a defeated, broken character of a bygone era.

CHAPTER SEVEN

Pablo Sala and Columbia Gardens

These are the Gardens of the Desert . . .

—WILLIAM CULLEN BRYANT, *The Prairies*

To see a world in a grain of sand and a Heaven in a wild flower,
Hold infinity in the palm of your hand
And eternity in an hour

—WILLIAM BLAKE

After acquiring the Zeringue plantation, Pablo Sala turned it into Columbia Gardens, a nightclub and pleasure resort. The roadside club was modeled after a similar venue called Whitehall or Suburban Gardens, located in the old de La Barre home on the east bank of the river at Central Avenue. Sala's role in the day-to-day operations of the resort is difficult to ascertain, but it is clear that his investment was worthwhile. The 1893 opening-day ceremonies were attended by one thousand guests.[1]

Visitors to Columbia Gardens rode a steamboat called the *Belle of the Coast* from the foot of Canal Street in New Orleans to the plantation. Captains Comeaux and Aikens commanded the steamer. Guests walked through the vast and immaculately kept gardens that surrounded the house and enjoyed the numerous flowers that grew there. In fact, the zealous promoters of the resort boasted that Columbia Gardens contained the "grandest flower garden in America."[2]

A generator on the grounds provided lights for the resort, which was one of the first structures on the west bank to boast electricity. Patrons marveled at the strands of electric lights that hung from the house and surrounding foliage. Changing lights flickered throughout the gardens, and the house glittered and sparkled from the flagstone-covered porch to the top of the belvedere. Above the front door of the plantation house hung a blazing star and horseshoe, both lit with electric lights. This illumination was a major marketing tool and was often promoted in advertisements in the *Daily Picayune*.[3]

The resort even boasted a tightrope walker, trapeze artists, and gymnasts in the gardens for the amusement of the guests. Other entertainers of all sorts regularly entertained guests. Inside the house, patrons danced to the music of the New Orleans Symphony and enjoyed songs by St. Theresa's Church Choir. The Continental Guard's Band also regularly provided music for dancing and performed a number of military marches, colorful processions, and ceremonies, sometimes accompanied by other military groups. Among the most popular performers to entertain at the resort was Jules Levy. An advertisement in an 1893 issue of the *Daily Picayune* stated, "Messrs. Comeaux and Aiken take great pleasure in announcing that they have succeeded in obtaining the services of the peoples' favorite, Jules Levy, the world's great cornetist! who will perform his beautiful and wonderful solos, which have delighted millions of people all over the world, as well as most of the crowned heads of Europe."[4]

Inside the house, promoters treated guests with ice cream, cakes, and champagne. Guests also used the resort for various sporting events and picnicked on the plantation grounds. Columbia Gardens was not only a major attraction in its own right but also the site of a number of special events sponsored by various social groups and organizations. For example, the May 24, 1893, issue of the *Daily Picayune* ran an advertisement for a "Grand Excursion" to Columbia Gardens sponsored by the Standard Benevolent Association to benefit its Relief Fund. The small advertisement boasted a ladies' foot race, a tug of war, a sparring contest, and a children's jumping contest. The association also sponsored a baseball game, J. J. Cliffords vs. E.J.H.B.C., as well as foot races for both exempt and active members of the organization. The steamer, *Belle of the Coast*, began transporting visitors from Canal Street at eight in the morning and continued shuttling them back and forth until eleven that evening. The Standard Benevolent Association held its excursion on Sunday, June 4, 1893, charging twenty-five cents for tickets and admitting children under seven for free.[5]

Columbia Gardens held one of its largest celebrations one month later, on July 4, 1893. The Patriotic Order Sons of America sponsored a large Independence Day celebration in which the Comeaux-Aiken Company shuttled twenty thousand people from Canal Street to Columbia Gardens. Four additional steamers transported the crowds across the Mississippi River. Among these extra boats were the *Mabel Comeaux*, the *Stella Wilds*, the *Jesse K. Bell*, and the *Thomas Pickles*.

This large celebration was heralded in extensive advertisements in the *Daily Picayune*. These advertisements boasted that there would be no crowding at the resort (although, twenty thousand people were surely quite a crowd). Furthermore, the advertisements boasted there were to be no inconveniences associated with the celebrations and stated, "Every arrangement has been perjected (sic) for the comfort of ladies and children entrusted to our care."

A number of guests met early in the morning that Independence Day at the Commercial Club, where club president Robert Bleakley welcomed them. A. B. Booth and R. J. Chauvin thanked the club for favors extended. Guests were then driven to the foot of Canal Street, where they met the five boats. A fee of fifteen cents covered the round-trip fare and entrance to the celebrations, where guests enjoyed a large presentation and ceremony that included patriotic music in honor of the nation's Independence Day. Musicians played "Yankee Doodle," "The Star Spangled Banner," "Nearer My God to Thee," and other songs. Company B of the Continental Guards made a colorful military display, and Revered Walter C. Pierce led the entire group in prayer.

Numerous sports and activities followed the ceremonies, including two baseball games: Fletchers vs. Memorys and Schotts vs. Milans. Amid all the amusements, guests enjoyed a large dinner followed by an impressive fireworks display described as "The most perfect and unique pyrotechnic display yet seen south." Independence Day 1893 ended with twenty thousand guests dancing on the grounds of the old plantation on immense platforms amid the illuminated garden.[6]

The plantation's success can be attributed to the interaction of several important factors. First, its location directly across the Mississippi River from New Orleans was ideal for a tourist attraction. A steamboat brought passengers from the foot of Canal Street (New Orleans's "main street") nearly to the plantation's front doorstep. It provided an area that was close to the city and extremely accessible, but at the same time, the resort was truly a world away. It was across the wide river, giving the impression of traveling to a distant locale.

Organizers provided low-cost, easily accessible, timely transportation in a widely enjoyed style. Although it was a short trip, riding a steamboat to the "wilds" of the west bank was certainly part of the thrill of the resort.

Organizers heavily promoted the venue, advertising almost daily in the newspaper. Big, bold advertisements in the *New Orleans Daily Picayune* ensured that many people knew about Columbia Gardens. The colorful wording and somewhat pushy headlines were designed to grab readers' attentions. The organizers promoted the location as a southern paradise. One advertisement stated, "NOW IS YOUR OPPORTUNITY to enjoy the cool, magnificent breezes up and down the river, listen to the best music while sitting beneath the grand, majestic and beautiful magnolia trees, inhaling the delicious perfumes." Such romantic and idealistic imagery was a major selling point and perhaps a crucial marketing technique that ensured crowds at the resort.

The plantation provided a much-needed haven from the busy, dirty city. At the turn of the century, New Orleans was a bustling metropolis, full of buildings and people, whereas Seven Oaks was located in the middle of vast agricultural fields, surrounded by natural and developed vegetation. The river, canal, and nearby bayous provided ample natural beauty for enjoyment and sport. The further development of Camille Zeringue's plantation gardens further added to the rural mystique of the resort.

The plantation's rural yet sophisticated built environment provided a dual nature to this getaway. Like many of the resorts of our own day, it allowed visitors the opportunity to "rough it" for a while in a natural environment and "commune with nature," while always being close to the standard comforts of the day and the big city. Also like many of the resorts of our time, Columbia Gardens offered something for everyone. Ladies could socialize and enjoy a drink in the parlors or the verandas (in opulent splendor) or listen to the music of a choir or other musicians while their husbands explored the vast wilderness, fished in the back bayous, or played a game of baseball in the rural fields. Meanwhile, children could be entertained in the garden by various circus-like acts, or swim in the river or play along the canal. In the evening, all could enjoy a spectacular performance together and marvel at the mansion strung in electric lights.

Additionally, the developers of Columbia Gardens did something very important; they continuously monitored popular entertainments of the era and made sure to bring these performers to the venue. Jules Levy and other popular performers drew big crowds.

Columbia Gardens truly offered patrons a plethora of entertainments and enjoyments. And its unique combination of easily accessible location, tremendous advertising, rural yet sophisticated built environment, timely and popular entertainment, variety of amusements, and affordability meant great success for Pablo Sala and his colleagues. The resort was indeed ahead of its time. Such multifaceted attractions did not routinely develop until much later, and the use of the mansion as a tourist attraction was very unusual prior to the turn of the century. During the plantation mansion's last days many hoped to see it become a tourist attraction again, but the plantation's earlier success in such a venture was easily forgotten by those opposed to this use.

As thousands of guests were enjoying Pablo Sala's magnificent resort, he was busy developing the area around the Company Canal. He sold the upper end of the plantation to the Pacific Dock Company and began organizing the land along the canal by subdividing it into lots. By 1892, the first plan of "Salaville" was completed, and 162 lots were advertised for sale. They sold slowly at first.

The next year, the church established by the former Zeringue slaves in Red Bean Row purchased two lots for a new church. The congregation, now known simply as True Vine, sent trustees Maddison Pawell, Martin Tilton, and Louis Moses to negotiate the transaction. Tilton also purchased a lot for himself next to the church. Interestingly, the congregation is still a vital part of the community, and many of its members count themselves among descendents of former Zeringue slaves. Although the church has moved from its original location, it still makes its home on Sala Avenue in the area originally planned by Pablo Sala.

By this time, the Company Canal Store was operating in the vicinity, providing general dry goods and food for the area. It was similar in scope to the plantation stores seen on many estates. These enterprises often represented a public meeting place where visitors to the area would go first and where locals of all ages would socialize and share local news (fig. 9.)[7]

Fig. 9. The Company Canal Store was located on the banks of the canal that Camille Zeringue developed. This store served a number of economic and social functions for the expanding community along the waterway. Photograph courtesy of Daniel P. Alario Sr., Westwego, Louisiana.

On October 1, 1893, a natural disaster changed Salaville forever. A fierce hurricane ravaged the settlement at Cheniere Caminada, a secluded island in the Gulf of Mexico west of present-day Grand Isle. The storm took the lives of many of the residents and totally destroyed everything in its path. Many of the homeless hurricane victims immediately sought refuge on the mainland and soon purchased lots in Sala's little canal-side community. The population of the little town grew quickly, and the new residents brought with them spirit and character that pervades the community to this day. Many of their descendents still call the area "home" today.

Salaville was truly the perfect settlement for the hurricane survivors. Many, fearing such storms, wanted to retreat from the Gulf Coast but also longed to be near the water to continue their livelihoods of fishing and trapping. Salaville provided affordable lots along the canal, a water transportation route to nearby swamps, marshes, and bayous for fishing and trapping. In addition, the settlement was near New Orleans but far enough away that the settlers wouldn't be bothered by the annoyances of urban life. It became the perfect haven for many from Cheniere Caminada now displaced by the hurricane.

Pablo Sala died in October 1894.[8] His sister, Maria Sala y Fabregas of Spain, inherited the plantation.[9] She expanded the "Salaville" community, creating one hundred lots that extended to the first bend of Bayou Segnette. She also constructed Laroussini and Louisiana Streets. This quickly growing settlement was the precursor to the present-day city of Westwego.[10]

It has often been said that Westwego was born on the Company Canal, and this certainly is the case, but the Company Canal itself was born at Seven Oaks, fathered by Camille Zeringue and preceded by an earlier, smaller canal whose history stretched back to colonial times. The history of Westwego is forever intertwined with the Company Canal, and the Company Canal is forever intertwined with the plantation, and it is for this reason that without Seven Oaks, there may have been no Westwego.

After Maria Sala y Fabregas died, ownership of the plantation passed to Narcisso Barres Durel on February 11, 1898; then it was sold to Alphonse A. Lelong in 1901. The following year Lelong sold it to his own land company, the A. A. Lelong Land and Improvement Association, Limited. Four years later, on May 29, 1906, Charles T. Soniat acquired the plantation. On April 24, 1912, he sold it to E. G. Merriam, a trustee of the Missouri and Pacific Railroad Company. The railroad now had full control of the property that Camille Zeringue had fought so long and hard to keep away from them.[11]

After Sala's death, as the plantation changed hands, Columbia Gardens closed its doors. Although the magical resort did not exist long, it was certainly a tremendously popular venue during its time. The "pleasure gardens" brought much wealth and industry to the area along with large numbers of tourists. Pablo Sala knew in the 1800s what today's citizens and politicians are "discovering"—what a prime spot the plantation area (today Westwego) is for tourism and the phenomenal economic growth that a strong local tourism industry can bring. Even after Columbia Gardens had closed it doors to visitors, its huge impact was still felt in the quickly expanding community.

As Columbia Gardens faded into history, the plantation house returned to its original intended use—to house a large family. One of the families that resided at Seven Oaks was the Giardinas. Brothers Guiseppe, Jacob, and Salvadore married three Piccone sisters. They were from Ustica, a small island off the coast of Sicily, and settled in Harvey on the west bank of the Mississippi River. The three couples moved into the Seven Oaks mansion a few years after the turn of the century with their children and occupied the mansion as well as many of the slave cabins. They lived there as tenant farmers, raising a variety of crops. The men farmed with mules, growing vegetables, which they transported to the French Market in New Orleans or sold to passing riverboats that stopped at the plantation.[12]

The Giardina family oral history recounts the lively times the large extended family had at Seven Oaks. Without a radio, they provided their own entertainment, and the piano was at the center. They also greatly enjoyed a magnificent orchard of orange, peach, and plum trees that surrounded the house.[13]

It is said that the Giardinas tried to purchase the plantation from the railroad, but, when the railroad would not sell, the family moved upriver to Waggaman. Salvadore and Giuseppe bought a farm site and split it in half. The area is still farmed by the family today.[14]

In 1912, the railroad offered the plantation for sale. Jefferson parish sheriff Louis H. Marrero Sr. was convinced by his son to purchase a section of the plantation. Marrero tried to purchase the mansion and a few acres surrounding it for his family; however, the railroad refused to sell the small piece of the property, wanting instead to sell the entire parcel. Later, in the 1940s, the Westwego Veterans of Foreign Wars post tried to purchase the mansion to restore it as a meeting hall. Again, the railroad refused to sell.[15]

CHAPTER EIGHT

A New War, a New Family

We had the privilege of living in two different generations. Our
lives were richer and fuller under the tender care of Seven Oaks.
Now it is all over.

—MILDRED STEHLE HARRIS

During World War I, the United States army used the large master house at
Seven Oaks Plantation as a barracks to house 150 enlisted men. These
troops guarded the crucial railroad lines.[1]

The railroad lines were very important to the war effort, and no chances
were taken with their protection. Not only did trains transport machinery
and supplies, they also transported donkeys and mules. These animals were
unloaded at the large railroad wharf and loaded onto ships that transported
them overseas. Because these animals were such good carriers, they were a
much needed addition to the war effort, and many made their way through
the plantation grounds en route to the war. Another important supply transported via the rail lines was cotton. Unlike donkeys and mules, cotton was a
major product seen on the wharf both in wartime and during peace. Often,
the wharf was so filled with huge bales of cotton that there was little room
available for the needed workmen.[2]

A memo from Major E. L. Higdon, the commanding officer of the 4th
Battalion of the United States Guards, was sent from Camp Beauregard,
Louisiana, to the Adjunct General of the Army in Washington, D.C., on
December 26, 1918. The subject of this memo was listed as "Historical Record
4th Battalion US Guards USA." The four-page, typed memo recounted that
the 4th Battalion of the U.S. Guards was organized at Camp Nicholls,
Louisiana, on May 26, 1918, per telegraphic instructions for Headquarters of

the Southeastern Department in Charleston, South Carolina. The memo further elaborates that "Company 'D' 4th Battalion US Guards was organized at Camp Nicholls, [Louisiana] August 11th, 1918, and consisted of four (4) Officers and one-hundred and fifty (150) Enlisted Men. A detachment of fifty (50) Enlisted Men Company 'D' 4th Battalion US Guards in command of 2nd Lieutenant Theodore H. Martin, left Camp Nicholls, La. August 12th, 1918, to take station at Westwego, La., relieving Det. 43rd Infantry, to guard T & P Railroad, wharves, and grain elevators, per Special Order #29 Headquarters 4th Battalion US Guards dated August 9th, 1918."[3]

During the soldiers' stay at Seven Oaks, the United States War Department made many modern improvements to the mansion. The military installed permanent electricity in the house for the men. Because there was no running water and outhouses were insufficient to provide for the needs of this large group, the United States Army constructed a latrine, complete with running water, for the soldiers. The structure itself was built about fifty feet away from the main house. It contained at least five pull-chain toilets, whose tanks rested high along the wall, and a shower facility for the men.

In order to accommodate such a large number of soldiers, the wide second-floor gallery surrounding the house was screened, and a number of cots were placed there. This served as a cool, dry sleeping area for many of the men and increased the living area of the mansion substantially. The large overhanging roof provided shade during the day. The screens allowed cool breezes to flow through the porch at night and also reduced the potential for contracting insect-borne diseases such as malaria. (See fig. 10.)[4]

Each improvement made to the mansion was countered by damage inflicted by the troops. The profusion of soldiers began the deterioration process that eventually consumed the old house. The black marble mantels from the dining room fireplaces and other fireplace mantels throughout the house were ripped out for unknown reasons. Some suggest that the soldiers sent the small pieces of imported marble home to their mothers, girlfriends, and wives as souvenirs of the time they spent in the antebellum mansion. They may also have taken them as souvenirs for themselves. Soldiers gouged holes in the walls and caused other extensive damage to the structure. The entire mansion felt the blow of such a large number of seemingly ungrateful guests.[5]

The United States military paid the railroad for the damages that occurred while its soldiers were stationed in the mansion; however, the railroad used

Fig. 10. The wide gallery of the Seven Oaks mansion surrounded the entire second story of the house. It functioned to keep the interior of the house cool. During World War I, the upper gallery was screened and used as sleeping quarters for 150 U.S. soldiers. Photograph by Angelo M. Rini Sr., courtesy of Angelo M. Rini Jr. and Charmaine Currault Rini, Gretna, Louisiana.

little of the money for repairs. It partially fixed some of the major damage. Railroad officials replaced the imported marble mantels with cheaper wooden ones, and much of the minor damage was never repaired at all.[6]

After the soldiers moved from the house, several families rented the great plantation mansion for their home, including the Taylors. Robert Taylor was employed by the company that leased the plantation property from the railroad. The company used the property to construct huge round oil storage tanks that sprouted up around the mansion, dotting the landscape between the magnificent oaks. Taylor was employed to oversee the

Fig. 11. A photograph of the mansion taken during the 1930s when Seven Oaks was rented as a private home. Photo by Richard Koch, courtesy of the Library of Congress, Prints & Photographs Division, HABS, Reproduction number HABS, LA, 26-WESWE, 1–4.

tanks, and it was essential that he remain close to them at all times. The company therefore allowed him and his family to live in the plantation mansion.[7] (See fig. 11.)

Robert Taylor's wife, Julia Therese Timpe, gave birth to two of her three children, Carl Timpe Taylor and Robert Taylor, in the plantation mansion.[8]

An older child, May, also resided there with her parents. The Taylor family shared the mansion with another family, each occupying one floor. This arrangement was fitting considering the size of the house and its architectural layout. The service stairs allowed those living on the second story to easily access their residence from the outside of the house without disturbing the family on the first floor. The Taylors lived at Seven Oaks for many years. Their family photographs showed the children enjoying the large yard surrounding the mansion and boys playing at the nearby railroad terminal. (See fig. 12.) The family then moved from the mansion to a smaller house nearby.[9]

Seven Oaks was also offered as a residence to George Persohn, a railroad grain inspector, and his family, soon after the turn of the century. George's wife, however, wanted to own her own property so that she would be free to grow a large garden. The family purchased property along the canal, and their possessions were shipped across the river on a wooden barge. The railroad offered another of its officials, William Howard Stehle, residence in the house, and he and his family accepted.[10]

In 1919, Stehle, along with his wife, Catherine Hoffman, and their four daughters, Irene, Mildred, Dorothy, and Marion, moved into the plantation house. The family may have shared the house earlier with the Taylors, but after Robert Taylor moved his family, the Stehles had the Seven Oaks mansion all to themselves.[11]

Mildred was only six years old when her family moved into the mansion. They had lived in a home on the east bank of the Mississippi River near Audubon Park. However, it was much more convenient for Stehle to live near the west bank wharves and elevators that he supervised. During this time the Huey P. Long Bridge that spans the Mississippi River between its east and west banks had yet to be constructed. Ferryboats provided the only transportation across the river.[12]

One of the first people the Stehles met after settling at Seven Oaks was a man named Celest, who lived on the property. He was a former slave, once owned by Camille Zeringue, and he maintained the grounds of the house, along with many other duties.[13] The family also came to rely on a man they called "Mr. Charlie." Mildred remembered that at night when the ferry stopped running, her family would stand on the levee and shout his name. Soon, he would appear in his little motorboat wearing a hat and

Fig. 12. Robert Sidney Taylor Jr. and his brother Carl Timpe Taylor play at the railroad terminal near their plantation home. Photograph courtesy of Carl A. Taylor, Marrero, Louisiana.

heavy coat. Often the entire family would squeeze into that little boat for a trip across the Mississippi River.[14]

Soon after the Stehles moved in, running water was installed in the mansion. Upstairs, carpenters closed sections of the large gallery near two of the bedroom doors and created two bathrooms. A small room under one of the staircases was remodeled to create a third bathroom.[15]

Mildred's first impression of the house was of its vastness. As a child she would often get lost in the huge home and have to call for her mother to rescue her: "The house was so big, and I was only seven years old, and we had just moved out of a small house into this great big mansion . . . A lot of times I would get upstairs and I wouldn't know which way to go to find the stairs. It was so that a child would get kind of confused."[16]

Mildred's childhood at Seven Oaks was a charmed one, highlighted by fun-filled afternoons playing in the old mansion. She and her sisters often played ball in the large upper gallery. They used a rolled up sock or stocking as the ball so their mother would not hear them. "The Stehle girls," as they were known in Westwego, also would run in the vast gardens surrounding the house. Mildred remembered playing outside with her sisters and finding large pieces of marble that at one time had been the beautiful, imported fire-place mantels. She remembered the various colors and types of marble: white, gray, and black. The girls would "play house" using the pieces of marble to construct little rooms or using the marble to "cook" on.[17]

The girls also loved to play in the mansion's belvedere. From this high point, they could see the Mississippi River from any direction they turned because Seven Oaks was situated near one of the river's dramatic curves. Mildred recalled how she and her sisters would open the large windows surrounding the room and how oblivious they were to the danger of falling out the windows from such a height. She also remembered being able to spot church steeples on St. Charles Avenue and other prominent structures in the skyline from the high vantage point.[18]

The sisters would sometimes dress in a hoop skirt and prance around the mansion, pretending they were the daughters of a wealthy planter in antebellum days. Mildred remembered the large metal hooks that pro-truded throughout the walls of the mansion and were used in early times to hang huge portraits or massive mirrors. The girls imagined whose enormous portraits had once hung on the large metal supports.[19]

Mildred, who considered herself a "tomboy," recalled how she and her sisters would use pieces of cardboard as a sled to coast down the levee near the house. They also played in the small ponds that would form between the levee and the riverbank after a heavy rain. One of the games the girls enjoyed most was hide-and-seek, which they played among the large bales of cotton after the business day had ended and the cotton wharves were vacant.

Mildred also recalled the immigrant farmers who leased part of the plantation property from the railroad. The Matranas, who immigrated from Sicily to Louisiana in 1900, leased 100 acres of land from the railroad. Nicolo Matrana and his wife, Rosario (Sarah), raised five sons on the grounds of the old plantation, where they established a small farm. Their youngest son, Frank (who later took over the farm), married Augustine Molaison, a descendent of the Zeringue family. Together, they had twelve children. Frank and Augustine lived on the farm until their deaths in 1979 and 1996, respectively. Frank Matrana Jr. still resides there with his family.

The Tripp family also established a farm on the grounds of the old plantation and grew such crops as tomatoes and okra. These two farming families had to cross the lawn of the mansion with their mules and wagons in order to make their way to the French Market in New Orleans to sell their produce. Mildred recalled the farmers stopping at her family's kitchen door to share their harvest. The farmers often brought corn, tomatoes, pumpkins, cantaloupes, and watermelons.[20]

Mildred also recalled the travelers and sightseers who often stopped at the mansion for directions, a meal, and even to spend the night at times. As crime was virtually unknown to the family members at the time, they had no qualms about letting strangers stay in the house. These "guests" often marveled at the mansion's size and beauty. It was not unusual to find artists on the lawn who had set up easels and were painting pictures of the house.[21] (See fig. 13.)

Such incidences give insight into the mansion's powerful appeal. It was the quintessential southern plantation house. Its rising columns and Greek Revival façade were what many envision when they think of a southern plantation mansion, and it was therefore a perfect model for amateur artists and masters alike. The big house's charm and historical significance summoned many visitors over the years, underscoring its prominent role as an important place in the community and the region.

Fig. 13. An artist's rendering in oil of Seven Oaks. The mansion inspired numerous works of art, and often painters with their easels could be found on the lawns. Image of painting courtesy of artist Betty L. Grummer, Colleyville, Texas.

During the time that the Stehles lived at Seven Oaks, the railroad leased property around the mansion to a petro-chemical company, which constructed huge petroleum storage tanks around the plantation house. During the construction of these tanks, crews unearthed the skeletal remains of six people. No evidence suggested that a formal cemetery existed on the spot where the skeletons were found; therefore, officials assumed that they had found the remains of slaves, soldiers, early settlers, or perhaps even the original Native American inhabitants of the area. Unfortunately, even after such a significant find, no formal archaeological investigations were suggested for the site.[22]

The skeletons were not the only artifacts found at Seven Oaks. The tenant farmers who settled vast fields of the old plantation reported finding impressive swords thought to have once belonged to Civil War soldiers or perhaps French or Spanish troops during the time that they occupied Louisiana before its statehood.

In a presentation to the Jefferson Historical Society of Louisiana, Mildred Stehle Harris recounted the story of a 1927 storm that threatened to flood the mansion. The Mississippi River nearly overflowed its levee, and William Stehle, being the railroad representative to the LaFourche Levee Board, had the immense responsibility of seeing that the levee remained intact. Stehle spent the entire night supervising the sandbagging of the levee in the area. Mildred, along with her mother and sisters, stayed behind in the mansion that night. As thunder crashed, lightning illuminated the dark night, casting eerie shadows through the house. "The trees became a mass of light" with each burst of lighting. The old house moaned and groaned. The Stehle girls and their mother prepared clothing, which they placed on a chair, in case they had to leave quickly during the night. Mildred remembered lying in bed that night, listening to the doors shake, the rain pour, and the wind whistle through the old oak trees, all the while wondering, *Will the night ever be over?* But, the wind grew stronger, and Mildred was surrounded by eerie, ghostly shadows cast from the knotty, entwined arms of an old oak tree. Frightening echoes and creepy noises besieged her, and the questions remained: *Will the levee give way? Will Father be safe? Will we all be drowned like rats?* The storm persisted, but the girls woke the next morning to the glorious news that the levee had not broken and everyone was safe. The Stehles had survived, and their century-old home was intact.[23]

One of Mildred's fondest memories of life at the plantation was of her senior dance. Mildred attended Westwego High School, which was then located in a small wooden building. Although only nine pupils made up Mildred's class, the town had no facility to hold the graduation dance, except the massive dining room at Seven Oaks. The students delighted in the news that the Stehles would open their home for the function. Mildred's older sister also had her class dance in the mansion at Seven Oaks.[24] (See fig. 14.)

Mildred recalled how the young men from her class went into the wilderness, gathered palmetto branches, and decorated the walls with them. The students hung Japanese paper lanterns all around and hung streamers in the class colors from the punkah on the ceiling. A jazz band played at one end of the dining room while the students danced the Charleston and Blackbottom at the other. The dance ended at midnight, and parents soon arrived to pick up their children.[25]

Another fond memory for Mildred was the marriage of her sister, Marion, which took place in the mansion. In preparation for the Creole-style wedding, the family erected an altar at one end of the dining room,

Fig. 14. Mildred Stehle (center, wearing plaid skirt) and her graduating class from Westwego High School. The Stehle family, who rented the house, allowed the seniors to hold their graduation dance in the dining room at Seven Oaks. Photograph courtesy of Daniel P. Alario Sr., Westwego, Louisiana.

decorated the house with white lilies and irises, and draped the staircase banisters with ivy. The bride descended the staircase, wearing a bouffant, Spanish-style dress made of white lace complimented by a mantilla. A music box that utilized copper disks played "Oh Promise Me" as the bride and her bridesmaids made their way into the dining room.[26]

Mildred attended college for two years in Natchitoches, Louisiana, on a Jefferson Parish Police Jury scholarship. She traveled to school on the train with a free pass because she was the daughter of a railroad employee. Mildred married Edwin C. Harris in 1943. The couple resided in the Seven Oaks mansion for eight years. During World War II, when their husbands went to war, the other Stehle girls returned home to Seven Oaks along with their families. After their husbands returned from the war front, the Stehle girls moved from the house—all except Mildred and Edwin. The couple remained at the mansion until Mildred realized she was pregnant with their second child.[27]

During her pregnancy, Mildred and Edwin built a home about a mile from the mansion. Mildred worked as a schoolteacher under principal Stella Worley for nineteen years at Westwego High School before becoming the principal of nearby Bridge City Elementary School. Mildred, a talented artist, began painting pictures of the old house that she would always call home. She never forgot her fond memories of growing up in a plantation mansion. She said, "It was a great house to live in. The house itself seemed to be a place where you could have fun and where you could enjoy [life]."[28]

William Stehle and his wife, Catherine, remained at Seven Oaks for three years after Mildred and her family moved. The roof starting leaking badly in a room that wasn't being used, and, finally, the plaster ceiling began to crumble. The railroad refused to repair the leak. By 1954 the leak had grown larger and forced the Stehles to move.[29]

CHAPTER NINE

The Mansion Begins to Fade

Man differs from the lower animals because he preserves
his past experiences.

—JOHN DEWEY, *Reconstruction in Philosophy*

Defaced ruins of architecture and statuary, like the wrinkles of
decrepitude of a once beautiful woman, only make one regret that one
did not see them when they were enchanting.

—HORACE WALPOLE

After the Stehle family moved from the old plantation house, it was left in
the care of the railroad, whose officials had no interest in historic preservation. Railroad executives, busy with the business of running a major transportation industry, abandoned Seven Oaks and left it forgotten. Without
inhabitants or caretakers, the house quickly deteriorated. During the late
1950s, preservationists prompted the American Liberty Oil Company,
which leased the site of the plantation from the Missouri-Pacific Railroad,
to preserve the structure. Sometime in 1957, the oil company, led by
President James J. Coleman, invested three thousand dollars in a temporary
roof on the old mansion in an attempt to help preserve it. The oil company
also cleaned the grounds surrounding the mansion, stabilized the structure,
and built a shell-lined drive from the main road to the house. Coleman
contacted the Louisiana Landmarks Society, and the organization became
actively involved in preservation efforts.[1]

Louisiana Landmarks Society president Leonard Huber summarized the
group's plans: "Our first objective is to make part of the house at least hab-
itable, then install caretakers and to charge visitors a nominal admission

Fig. 15. Seven Oaks Plantation, front view. Note barrel-like cistern on the side of the house, and oil storage tanks in the left background. Photograph by Richard Koch, courtesy of the Library of Congress, Prints & Photographs Division, HABS, Reproduction number HABS, LA, 26-WESWE, 1–9.

fee, using the proceeds to gradually restore the whole building to its original form." The society sponsored a "Fête Champetre" on Sunday, April 14, 1957, in order to raise funds to restore the house. On May 5 of the same year, the society held another event, a free open house, at which the public could preview the mansion. Noted architectural historian and scholar Samuel Wilson Jr., who had surveyed the plantation house for the Historic American Buildings Survey (HABS), spoke at the event, which, because of good publicity and favorable weather, was attended by two to three thousand individuals.[2]

On the following Sunday, Coleman and the American Liberty Oil Company opened the house again to the public. In an article in *Dixie* magazine, Coleman was quoted as saying, "Initially the company leased only the land on which the tanks are located . . . The house on adjacent land, as you notice was vacant and decaying rapidly. I didn't want to see a dying landmark like Seven Oaks disappear, so I arranged for the firm to lease the land it's on, too . . . The lease for the land beneath the house gives me permission to do what I want to with the mansion. I could tear it down because the land is a valuable commercial site. But when I was a child

I used to ride on the highway in front of the house. It fascinated me then and fascinates me now. I want to do everything I can to preserve that house, not tear it down."[3]

Coleman made it clear that he was willing to work with any individual or organization interested in restoring the house for the public on a non-profit basis. He even offered to try to purchase the house and donate it to such a group. Preservation efforts seemed to be going well, but behind the scenes turmoil lurked. At a meeting of the Board of the Louisiana Landmarks Society on June 4, 1958, it was decided that the organization would disassociate from financing the restoration of Seven Oaks. The reasons for this prompt withdrawal were not clearly stated to the public, but the board noted that the American Liberty Oil Company's twenty-five-year lease prevented a serious financial investment by the society. The society was uncertain of its role and the ultimate fate of the house when the oil company's relatively short lease expired. If the oil company continued leasing the property, the plantation's fate and the society's principal part in it would probably be assured; however, if the railroad did not renew the company's lease or if it found a new lessor, the society's efforts and financial contributions could very well be compromised. No one stepped forward to meet Coleman's offer, and the excitement over preservation of the house seemed to wane.[4]

Without the Louisiana Landmarks Society's full financial support, Seven Oaks was again left to deteriorate as the years passed. By the 1960s, it is said that beverage cans, pieces of automobiles, and other litter were scattered about the floors, which had been seriously vandalized. Storms and hurricanes hastened the decay of the mansion. In 1965, Hurricane Betsy, which ravished much of the area, caused great damage to the mansion. The hurricane ripped the belvedere from the house and slammed a giant tree branch into the house, damaging a large portion of the roof.[5]

Even in a deteriorated state, the mansion was a popular spot for young lovers. Journalist Herschel Miller witnessed the graffiti that decorated the walls: "Like a sign of our times, a suggestion that one civilization has encroached on another, on the walls have appeared the ignorant scrawls of the graffiti writers, bringing to the handsome old rooms words that for centuries have been the exclusive property of public latrines."[6]

Treasure hunters often visited the house, digging holes in the floors and lifting floorboards in search of hidden riches. Rumors emerged of treasure secretly concealed in the plantation mansion's thick walls. The fourteen-inch-thick walls only made matters worse, offering plenty of space for imaginary treasure to hide, especially in the minds of those who believed it was there. These treasure hunters also tore into the walls seeking hidden passageways or secret rooms. There were no hidden passages, no secret rooms, and no hidden treasure. Sadly, the greatest treasure, the mansion itself, was ripped apart in vain by those blindly seeking wealth.[7]

Vandals also visited the site, destroying a piece of Louisiana's heritage for the pure fun of it. Vandals carved obscenities and punched holes into the walls, destroying many of the exterior French doors and interior doors, and ripped out mantels throughout the house.[8]

Along with the thrill-seeking vandals, the wealth-seeking hunters, and fun-seeking youngsters came the ill-fated homeless, who, in seeking shelter, made the once great mansion their home and caused even more damage to the house. Finally, there were the sentimental locals and tourists alike, who only wanted a souvenir from the mansion. They carried away what was left of the house: the doorknobs, the hardware from the French doors and windows, what remained of the staircase, and anything else they could remove. The mansion lay stripped and damaged, but even then, preservation and restoration could still have taken place with some effort.[9]

In 1969, Herschel Miller wrote in *New Orleans Magazine* about the damage he had seen at Seven Oaks and the indifference of some of the people who lived around the mansion all their lives. "Betsy tore gaping holes in the roof, tossed the old cypress beams around like kindling, but perhaps more important than the physical damage it inflicted, like a benevolent act of God, it provided a convenient rationale, a slave for the conscience, for it is said that after Betsy, it was impossible to do anything for Seven Oaks. Perhaps this is the greater damage of Betsy to Seven Oaks, for this mortal wound, in all its convenient aspects, serves to obscure and pass forgiveness on the half-century that it stayed unattended, save by those who passed to gape and wreck and vandalize, and among others, by those who found nocturnal pastimes in its rooms, and in a lurid afterglow to scrawl remembrances on the old plaster walls."[10] (See figs. 16a, 16b, 16c.)

In 1967, there was again a great effort to save the plantation. Arthur Dahlman, general manager of the A. J. Toups Contracting Company, proposed a reconstruction of the plantation house on land to be donated by

Fig. 16(a–c). The interior of the house faced damage from weather, vandals, and other sources, but the structure's beauty, history, and integrity remained evident. Photographs by Richard Koch, 1965, courtesy of the Library of Congress, Prints & Photographs Division, HABS, Reproduction number HABS, LA, 26-WESWE, 1–11, 1–12, 1–13.

Jefferson Parish. The parish council backed the idea of constructing an exact replica of the house. Research determined that such a replica could be constructed using much of the original materials at a cost of half a million to a million dollars. Dahlman and his company offered to take full financial

Fig. 16b.

responsibility for the project. Dahlman planned to open a restaurant, a souvenir shop, and a dance hall. He recruited Richard C. Moledous to head the architectural duties of the project.[11]

Many people voiced objections to Dahlman's idea of re-creating a piece of history. These people urged preservation and restoration rather than replication. Bethlyn McCloskey, chairman of the Jefferson Parish Advisory

Fig. 16c.

Board on Environmental Development, commented that the board would much rather see an authentic ruin than a fabrication. Like other efforts, this failed, and all the while the mansion deteriorated more and more. Vandals and treasure hunters continued to tear away at the mansion. The railroad allowed all these people to run rampant, destroying everything in sight, until officials realized that the ruins created a safety hazard. At that point, railroad officials installed a fence around the mansion to protect themselves from lawsuits. Of course, those who wanted to creep inside the ruined mansion found a way around, over, or under the fence.

Now the great mansion was only a shell of its original grandeur. Vines and grass covered the remainder of the fourteen-inch-thick brick walls. The windows and doors had been removed. Hurricanes and storms stripped the mansion of its roof, along with its four chimneys, eight dormer windows, and impressive belvedere. The once great plantation house now stood in ruins. Even though the harsh elements stripped the massive columns naked of their smooth plaster, exposing their brick foundation, they still stood dignified and proud. The house itself, now only a shadow of what it once was, still radiated a commanding presence, restrained and elegant.

As the mansion continued to deteriorate, the railroad ignored the cries of thousands of people who wished to see the mansion preserved. The Louisiana Landmarks Society, preservationists, and ordinary citizens pleaded with the railroad to do something—anything—to preserve this crucial piece of Louisiana history and part of our national heritage. Many individuals and groups even offered their assistance. The railroad, however, remained indifferent.

Few realized at the time that the mansion was located in a prime spot for tourists. The only other plantation mansion that existed that could possibly compare with Seven Oaks was Oak Alley in Vacherie, fifty-nine miles to the west. Seven Oaks stood only one mile from the Huey P. Long Bridge, almost directly across the river from Audubon Park, and was quite easily accessible from downtown New Orleans. If restored, the mansion would have been an unmatched tourist attraction of this type and would have provided a great deal of revenue for the City of Westwego and rapidly growing Jefferson Parish. But neither the railroad nor the City of Westwego, or even Jefferson Parish, had the foresight (or hindsight) necessary to envision Seven Oaks once again as a bustling tourist mecca. Although it once served as a popular attraction in the area, this fact seems to have been quickly and conveniently forgotten.

But, even in its ruined, fading state, Seven Oaks' charm continued to capture the attention of many. In 1973, the ruins of the once splendid mansion received one of its most famous visitors when prominent playwright and author Truman Capote went to the location for a photo shoot. Capote, who was born in New Orleans, was best known for his fictional works such as *Breakfast at Tiffany's*, *In Cold Blood*, and *The Grass Harp*. Southern settings provided the backdrop for many of the award-winning writer's works.

Don Lee Keith, an ace feature writer for the *Times-Picayune*, interviewed Capote and planned the photo shoot at Seven Oaks. In order to land the interview, he wrote a long letter to the author. Capote is said to have called Keith, pretending to be his own secretary. The newspaperman recognized Capote's distinctive voice but humored the writer by playing along with his game. This paid off, and Keith gained access to Capote.[12]

Keith meticulously worked out every detail of the photo shoot at Seven Oaks. A New York freelance photographer, Nicolas Sapieha, flew into New Orleans because Keith believed that no local photographer was good enough for the subject. Keith even hired a retired Pullman porter, Luther Houze, to serve champagne to Capote. Luther Houze thought the situation was a little more than strange. He told Keith that he never served at Seven Oaks before; Keith explained to him that Seven Oaks was the ruins of a once great plantation mansion. Houze then told Keith that he had never heard of having a party at a torn-down old place like that before. Despite his objections, Houze took the job. Keith then arranged for a young acquaintance, David Hughes, to assist the photographer.[13]

The photographer, along with his fifteen-year-old assistant and Houze, arrived at the plantation an hour early. After much preparation, the trio was ready for Capote. Keith soon arrived with Capote in tow; when Capote saw the ruins, he asked Keith if the decrepit surroundings were meant to represent his mind or his spirit. Keith answered that the ruins were meant to mirror his own condition, rather than Capote's.

The floorboards in the house were all vandalized and scattered about, making walking around the rooms a dangerous feat. Nevertheless, amid the ruins sat a small table covered in a starched white linen tablecloth. A silver tray, crystal champagne glasses, expensive champagne on ice, and a single rose in a crystal bud vase, sat on the little table. Houze, dressed in a tuxedo, stood next to the table, waiting to serve the writer his champagne. As he crept into the mansion, Capote asked if there were snakes in the house. "Many" someone answered.

After the first few rolls of film had been shot, Capote grew anxious and bored; he began to look at his watch. The writer complained of an upset stomach, but Keith persisted and Capote stayed. After nearly two thousand shots had been taken of Capote amid the ruins, Keith ushered the writer out.[14]

Certainly, the exhausting Capote photo shoot was an interesting note in the plantation's multifaceted history. Even in its decay, Seven Oaks held an attraction for Don Lee Keith and his readers. The house was like Capote himself, a southern treasure shaped by the culture and history of the region.

To its railroad owners, Seven Oaks meant very little, not even enough to warrant upkeep. However, the house held significantly more value to the surrounding community and wider region. Even abandoned, the plantation mansion attracted sightseers and enterprise. The photo shoot was just one example of how the house beckoned visitors and represented more than bricks and stucco. Artists and architects often visited the house to gain inspiration from its fading façade. Tourists and locals went to the plantation too for various symbolic reasons—to relive a part of history, to partake in the popular romantic, yet totally biased, legends of the old South, and even to try to capture in some way the ever-enduring and tempting storybook ideas of ghosts and the supernatural. Correctly, the mansion represented slavery but also the spirit of survival, the ability of the slaves of long ago to transcend their shackled existence and strive toward something greater. To its tormentors the mansion was an easy victim, whose crumbling walls offered little defense against vandalism and little risk for perpetrators of being caught. In whatever way it was symbolic, it was also important—important to many individuals and the larger community alike.

Seven Oaks represented many things to many people, and, in order to understand the plantation's twentieth-century history, it is important to realize that its late lure was as significant as its earlier lore. And it was these alluring qualities that fueled the fiery political battles over the plantation's fate that were yet to come.

CHAPTER TEN

Save Seven Oaks

If something isn't saved, then what's it all for?

—SYDNEY POLLACK

Architecture is life, or at least it is life itself taking form and therefore it
is the truest record of life as it was lived in the world yesterday, as it is
lived today or ever will be lived.

—FRANK LLOYD WRIGHT, *AN ORGANIC ARCHITECTURE*

Through the years, the mansion at Seven Oaks lay abandoned and neglected. During that time, it continued to deteriorate, fading away more rapidly as the years passed. In November 1975, a Westwego city attorney ordered the Texas-Pacific-Missouri-Pacific Railroad to repair the crumbling Seven Oaks mansion or demolish it. This order soon led to a fierce battle between those opposing the demolition of the master house and those who wanted it demolished. Preservation efforts were increased, and many grassroots efforts began to try to save Seven Oaks from demolition.[1]

In February 1976, the Westwego Board of Aldermen condemned the ruined structure and ordered it to be demolished. The elected aldermen were tired of the "eye-sore" amid the industrial tanks and feared possible lawsuits. They hoped the demolition order would end the problem.

With this, there was an even greater call to save the building. Westwego mayor Ernest Tassin's office quickly filled with letters that urged preservation and restoration of the historic home. Telephone lines at Westwego City Hall also rang constantly, with the great majority of calls pleading for the city to save Seven Oaks.[2]

Betsy Swanson, author of *Historic Jefferson Parish From Shore to Shore*, wrote one of the letters that the mayor received. Swanson featured the plantation in her book and deplored the demolition of the mansion in the nation's Bicentennial year. She begged the city to make an effort at least to preserve the remains of the mansion, without necessarily restoring the building itself.

By stabilizing the structure and removing debris, the city would spend much less than needed for a complete restoration while providing a safe setting for people to view the ruins. Swanson suggested that the city create a park-like setting around the ruins, which would provide a much-needed recreation site, an attractive setting for what was left of the mansion, and a tourist attraction for Westwego and Jefferson Parish. The deterioration of the structure would then be halted, and future restoration could be undertaken at a more appropriate time.[3]

This was an especially interesting suggestion as the ruins of the plantation were even then attracting tourists. The fence around the mansion provided only a weak deterrent as those who wanted to get closer readily did. A ruins park would not only have allowed the structure to be preserved for future restoration but would have provided a unique public facility. Although many plantation homes throughout the South have been preserved, very few ruins have been preserved. Those that have been, such as Windsor Plantation in Mississippi, typically contain only the remaining columns of the buildings. Seven Oaks would have, perhaps, been a one-of-a-kind attraction in America, a complete crumbling mansion halted in it deterioration. Unlike Europe, which is full of ruins—many attracting millions of tourists each year—America has very few ruins of its relatively short past. Seven Oaks opened publicly, even as ruins, would have surely continued to attract much attention and many additional tourists.

The mayor of Westwego felt quite bitter about the negative responses he received concerning the future demolition of Seven Oaks. He asked where all these people were when the city tried to preserve the building fifteen years before, when Westwego officials tried to get the plantation on the National Register of Historic Places. Tassin said that no one came to the aid of Seven Oaks until the council condemned it. The mayor explained that a New Orleans attorney offered to put up half a million dollars for the restoration of the mansion, but the city was no longer interested in restoration or preservation and apparently turned down the generous offer.

Westwego's main concern continued to be the potential lawsuits that might result if someone was injured while in the ruins. Mayor Tassin said, "We tried to get Seven Oaks into the federal registry of historic landmarks, but nobody came to our aid until we ordered the building condemned and demolished. We are not looking for any money and do not want the responsibility of restoring the building. Our concern right now is . . . the possibility of lawsuits, which might result from somebody being injured in those ruins."[4]

At this time, city officials focused on the plantation mansion as a liability. They saw the house as a deteriorating old structure that could potentially cost the city money if a far-fetched civil court ruling favored the plea of a theoretical trespasser injuring himself. What to do with this liability was a much more difficult problem for these city officials. Restoration or even preservation would be very costly. These elected leaders saw the immense cost involved in pursuing the conservation of the mansion, not the possible gains for the community or the inevitable return on their initial investment. This view is not surprising given that such historic tourism was not as popular or pervasive as it is today, especially in the areas outside the New Orleans city limits. Whereas today local officials are pouring millions of dollars into the development of a tourist hub near the location of the plantation site, in the 1970s, tourism was the furthest thing from the local political agenda. But despite their reservations, leaders were persuaded at least to humor the whims of their constituents.

The next month the City of Westwego granted preservationists a one-month stay of execution—one last chance to save the dying mansion. Finally, Jefferson Parish's governing council, also hearing the pro-preservationist sentiment of local voters, pitched its hat into the preservation movement. Bruce D. Burglass Sr., Jefferson Parish Attorney, said, "We're going to try to do everything we can to preserve it as a tourist attraction." Burglass spoke bluntly, "The tragedy of this situation is that once you put a bulldozer to that place, there's nothing you can do."[5]

The Jefferson Parish Council created the seven-member Jefferson Parrish Historical Commission on March 4, 1976. The council established the commission to oversee historical projects, create a historical society, and promote parish history. One of the commission's primary goals was to work with the Office of the Parish Attorney to investigate how the parish might play a role in the preservation of the Seven Oaks mansion. Meanwhile, several historical and preservation groups contacted the parish government requesting assistance in the restoration and preservation of this crucial landmark.

Jefferson Parish Council chairman Charles J. Eagan Jr. noted that it would be difficult for the parish to give any assistance because Seven Oaks was located within Westwego city limits.[6] His statement was odd, and perhaps a forewarning of the parish's future disinterest in the project, as the parish government is often involved in public works within municipal city limits. But despite his reservations, the council did make some efforts to investigate what could be done for Seven Oaks.

By March 20, 1976, Jefferson Parish leaders met with officials from the Texas-Pacific-Missouri-Pacific Railroad to discuss the possibility of saving Seven Oaks. Railroad executives agreed to cooperate with parish officials in the preservation of the mansion but further added that they would not donate the land or structure for preservation and that they would not lease it at a token rate. At this point, the parish was faced with alternatives, such as outright purchase of the property. Railroad officials would allow the parish to purchase the land at about one dollar per square foot or between $40,000 and $50,000 per acre. The parish also had the option of subleasing the property from the primary lesser, North American Trading and Import Company, with the consent of the owner.[7]

Also, during the same week, Louisiana senator James H. Brown, chairman of the Joint Legislative Committee on Public Works, sent a letter to Westwego mayor Ernest Tassin offering the assistance of his committee and staff. The senator offered to look into the possibility of state and federal funds being made available for the preservation project. Brown called for an extended delay in demolition until his committee could meet to discuss the project. The committee was no stranger to the preservation effort, having worked to save historically significant sites throughout Louisiana.

The letter stated, "I think in a project like this, there is a possibility of some state funding that might be made available . . . I would certainly be willing to work with your legislators in Jefferson to bring something like this about. In addition, our committee is certainly willing to call on officials from the Missouri Pacific Railroad in an effort to enlist their cooperation . . . I might suggest an extended delay in any demolition efforts, and I would immediately call a special meeting of our joint legislative committee to consider what federal and state funding might be available. I will also make available to you members of our research staff to look over the entire area in hopes of saving the structure."[8]

Things were beginning to look up for Seven Oaks. By the end of the month, the Jefferson Parish Council chairman reported that parish officials were much closer to leasing the site of the mansion than they had been earlier in the month. The parish planned to stabilize the ruins at a cost of about $100,000, which would allow for a total restoration in the future.[9]

State Representative Sam LeBlanc III, also an attorney for North American Trading and Import Company, announced that his client, the lessee of the Seven Oaks site, would sublease the three or four acres surrounding the mansion. LeBlanc added that company officials believed that the restoration of the mansion would be in the best interests of the people of Jefferson Parish and the state of Louisiana.[10]

From the beginning of the struggle to save Seven Oaks, many preservationists fought diligently, but one voice could be heard distinctively over the others: that of State Representative John A. Alario Jr. from Westwego. Alario pushed for the preservation of Seven Oaks and tried to convince his fellow members of the House that preserving this piece of history was the right thing to do. Alario had been a lifelong resident of the area, his family being prominent and influential in the vicinity. While he surely had emotional ties to the old Seven Oaks mansion, he also clearly saw potential resting in the ruins. Alario, who later served several terms as Louisiana Speaker of the House, held a steadfast and unyielding belief in the promise that preservation held for this plantation.

In April 1976, Jefferson Parish officials authorized an application to acquire a $100,000 federal grant from the Community Development Innovative Project Program of the U.S. Department of Housing and Urban Development (HUD) to fund the preservation and stabilization of the mansion. The same week, Representative Alario announced that Louisiana governor Edwin W. Edwards had committed himself to spend up to $750,000 to acquire and restore the mansion. Alario announced his plans to turn the restored mansion into a state office building to house the driver's license bureau and other such state offices. Alario said, "The state would then maintain the property, so we would never again have to worry about it running down."[11]

Hearing Alario's idea of turning Seven Oaks into a state office building, some members of the Jefferson Parish Council began to question the project. The oil storage tanks that surrounded the plantation concerned Councilman Beauregard H. Miller Jr. He felt that they were a hazard that jeopardized the safety of visitors. Miller stated that he was in favor of preserving the plantation as a historical site; however, he was convinced safety should be a priority. Sensing the opposition of some of the council members, Chairman Eagan withdrew his resolution that would have allowed the parish to aid the state in negotiating the acquisition of the site. It was this type of local political bureaucracy and general lack of governmental synchrony that thwarted preservation efforts time and time again.

It is particularly interesting to note Councilman Miller's reservations regarding the location of the tanks in proximity to the mansion. The tanks were indeed quite close to the mansion, but whether they posed a threat to visitors is questionable. What is remarkable to mention is that the house was no longer seen as occupying a relatively rural, parklike setting as it did when Pablo Sala found success with Columbia Gardens. Much of the success of this resort relied on its location, including its perceived seclusion in a scenic and natural recreational area. Now the plantation was surrounded by oil storage tanks, in a fenced industrial area, which begs the question, "Can industry coexist with an historic attraction?" This was certainly one of the major concerns of many, and question lingered for the rest of the mansion's days.

On April 13, 1976, the *Times-Picayune* reported that Mayor Ernest Tassin of Westwego, and the Board of Aldermen officially endorsed the concept of restoring the Seven Oaks mansion as a public facility. The resolution, which reserved the right to review and ratify any final agreements, gave Jefferson Parish the authority to take "any and all necessary preliminary action, including negotiations, for the purchase of Seven Oaks Plantation and approximately 5 acres of ground."[12]

On the same day, the *Times-Picayune* also ran a story concerning State Representative Alario's response to the Jefferson Parish Council's opposition to aiding the state with negotiations to acquire the mansion. The newspaper quoted Alario as saying, "It appears that if a project is designed to help Westwego and the Fifth Ward, the council can find all kinds of excuses to delay and try to defeat its completion." Alario also responded to the comments made by Councilman Miller in which he questioned the safety of citizens who might visit the restored mansion. Alario assured the council that safety remained a priority. "The state is going to take every precaution to make sure Seven Oaks is safe for anyone wanting to visit it— even councilmen." Representative Alario went on to say that, "Taking a preservation project before the Jefferson Parish Council is like having Colonel Sanders baby-sit for your chickens." His obvious frustration with the situation further illustrated his commitment to the plantation's preservation, as well as his emotional ties to the project. One of the state's greatest historical treasures had not only been allowed to deteriorate but had also been set for demolition, and many people shared Alario's dismay.[13]

Alario presented his idea of restoring Seven Oaks to the Louisiana House of Representatives. He petitioned for an amendment to the capital outlay program that would have provided $750,000 for the restoration of the mansion. The project failed by a 43-to-42 vote. Many legislators felt that the state did not have the money to restore the mansion. A second amendment, which sought $75,000 for the project, also failed by a 40-to-40 vote.[14]

Westwego leaders, along with preservationists, met with officials from the Texas-Pacific-Missouri-Pacific Railroad. Although many talks commenced, the railroad refused to sell the site. Railroad vice-president Charles Roberts believed that a restored historic site would compromise the industrial area surrounding the mansion. Alario then tired to convince Governor Edwards to expropriate the property, but the governor refused such a drastic act.[15]

Alario continued his fight to save the mansion by taking his ideas to the Senate Finance Committee. This, too, was unsuccessful. But despite setbacks, Alario refused to give up. He moved forward with one of the most creative political actions of his long and celebrated political career, when he proposed the creation of a Jesse James Memorial Site at the mansion. In doing this, he simultaneously sought to make the point that many of his colleagues did not read the resolutions before voting on them. The *Times-Picayune* reported that many viewed Jesse James as a modern-day Robin Hood, except for the railroads that he robbed. Alario's resolution read, "the notorious train robber of history perpetrated no worse evils upon the railroads of the country than the Texas-Pacific-Missouri-Pacific Terminal Railroad is perpetrating by its refusal to allow this great historic landmark and symbol of Louisiana's past to be preserved." Because there are so many of these types of resolutions, legislators usually simply glance at them before voting, and, therefore, they usually pass. This time Senator Anthony Guarisco of Morgan City read some of the resolutions, including Alario's attempt to save the mansion. He immediately brought the resolution to the attention of his fellow lawmakers, and the resolution was rewritten. Alario sent the resolution back to the House of Representatives and asked the State Park Commission to study the feasibility of acquiring the property and restoring it.[16]

In September 1976, Representative Alario announced that the federal government had denied funds for restoration or preservation of Seven Oaks. United States Representative Lindy Boggs brought Alario the news that the U.S. Department of Housing and Urban Development had rejected the application for funds under its Innovative Projects Program in Neighborhood Preservation. HUD stated that the project showed lack of innovation because similar projects had already been funded. The weak organization of the restoration project as well as lack of funding available on the parish and local levels did not impress HUD officials either. HUD also questioned how the mansion would be sustained at the end of the restoration.[17]

Although many of HUD's statements were valid points, the federal government's lack of support for the project was yet another literal, symbolic, and moral defeat in the battle for the plantation's preservation. It seems from this point the political situation took a turn from what appeared to be a positive environment for possible restoration to something completely malign. All the while, Alario continued his bold efforts.

The issue of preservation of the plantation mansion was then scheduled to go before the Louisiana Department of Art, Historical, and Cultural Preservation. Only eight days after Representative Boggs brought the news that the federal government refused to fund the restoration or preservation of Seven Oaks, local newspapers ran articles depicting the Jefferson Parish Council turning its back on the mansion. The council voted 3-to-2 defeating a resolution by Councilman James E. Lawson Jr. that would have allowed Jefferson Parish to support efforts to have the mansion placed on the National Register of Historical Places. Lawson believed that by placing the plantation house on the national register, the Jefferson Parish Council might receive federal funds for the project. Councilman Miller argued that federal funds would most likely only be allotted to match local funds used for the project.[18]

Councilman Lloyd F. Giardina, a descendent of the Giardinas who lived at Seven Oaks, explained the council's dilemma. "There was just no money," he said. "We had priorities . . . we were just realizing that our infrastructure was woefully inadequate. We didn't have drainage. We had wastewater treatment problems." Giardina further elaborated by explaining that the parish realized the need for drainage after a major flood. There had been no significant flooding for some years, and the parish was unaware of how serious the drainage problems were. Therefore, the council put nearly all its efforts and funds into solving these problems. Additionally, he said that, parishwide, the public was more interested in building parks and playgrounds for children than in preserving a plantation in Westwego. This left the council in an awkward position, with little choice but to prioritize its funds and efforts, and, sadly, saving Seven Oaks could not take precedence over the other major concerns.[19]

Complicating problems was the total lack of vision on the part of many local leaders. Seven Oaks was not the majestic, powerful political symbol of wealth and prosperity it once was but instead a crumbling monstrosity. Certainly local citizens felt strong emotional ties to this fading gem, but even most of those people saw the house as somewhat of a novelty, a relic from the past to be gently enjoyed and leisurely explored. Few, with the exception of Representative Alario and primary supporters, could see beyond this veil of apathy toward the plantation's exciting economic potential. In the public realm, the plantation was no longer associated with making money but rather with costing money. The economic impact of Columbia Gardens, the successful resort attraction, had long since been forgotten. No one remembered the throngs of thousands who made this venue a success during the attraction's late-nineteenth-century zenith. No one remembered the economic boom the house and its environs brought to the area long before debates about its future raged.

Lingering was the ultimate question of whether a publicly accessible historic structure could coexist with a surrounding industrial enterprise. Whereas Columbia Gardens had the benefit of a mostly natural, rural area, the plantation was now surrounded by massive rusty storage tanks. Perhaps the

romance of the plantation needed a larger rural setting to make it historically convincing to visitors.

But, in the case of Seven Oaks, the nature of encroaching industry did not
significantly limit the potential the plantation held. The storage tanks were
silent. They saw little human presence, and virtually no loud industrial
processes were associated with them. Petroleum products were moved periodically to and from the tanks, and maintenance was routinely performed.
Otherwise, these large tanks were motionless, lacking the environmental
annoyances often associated with other types of industrial enterprises.
Furthermore, much of the natural beauty of the site had actually been maintained; the giant oaks and other trees and sprawling green space were
untouched. The tanks and fences could have been cleverly minimized by pre-
cise and well-planned landscaping. Vines could have easily covered fences,
and large bushes and other plantings could have at least partially obscured the
tanks from view. A few of the closer tanks could have been moved if they presented any real safety hazard. This would have been a small price to pay for
preserving a community's heritage. It seems at least in theory that Seven Oaks
could have existed harmoniously with its close industrial neighbor, causing
little harm to the business and providing a great tourist attraction for the area.

On November 6, 1976, the *New Orleans States Item* reported that although
Westwego's Board of Aldermen was scheduled to meet again to vote on the
demolition of the mansion, another player entered the game to save Seven
Oaks. Obviously seeing the plantation's potential amid the tanks, Joseph
Marcello, owner of Elmwood Plantation restaurant immediately across the
river in nearby Harahan, stated that he was exploring the possibility of using
the mansion, either the ruins or a restored version, as a restaurant. Hearing
this, preservationists again called for yet another stay of execution.[20]

A few days later, the Westwego Board of Aldermen heard addresses from
historian and author Betsy Swanson and her fellow preservationists Mary
Louise Christovich and Bethlyn McCloskey, who were in favor of delaying
demolition of the mansion. Swanson gave a film presentation to the board
that showcased preserved ruins around the world, often famed for their aes-
thetics and their ability to attract tourists. Sawnson said, "Seven Oaks is
one of the loveliest ruins in Louisiana."[21]

Christovich explained to the board that she had tried to contact the
officials from the Texas-Pacific-Missouri-Pacific Railroad many times but

failed to reach them. She stated that because this company was based out of town, officials did not have local interests at heart; they came to Louisiana with little regard for the important historical relics of the area. Christovich was obviously correct in this observation, as the great majority of preservation supporters were locals who shared an emotional tie to the plantation mansion and property and also a wider vision of its potential impact as a tourist attraction.[22]

Louisiana governor Edwin W. Edwards telephoned in his request for the board to grant a stay of execution. Soon after, preservationists rejoiced as Westwego aldermen voted unanimously to delay providing the railroad with a demolition permit for six months. Westwego mayor Ernest Tassin said that he hoped that Christovich, McCloskey, and Swanson could persuade the railroad to cooperate in preservation efforts. Tassin also said that Governor Edwards would meet with officials from the Texas-Pacific-Missouri-Pacific Railroad to devise a plan for saving the mansion. The mayor further added, "The railroad said then that it was not interested in selling the property . . . All they said was that it was expensive commercial property, but they're not using it for anything. It's just overgrown with weeds, and the area up there is just an eyesore to the whole community."[23]

The six-month delay came and went, but no real plans for saving the mansion were adopted. On the last day, the Texas-Pacific-Missouri-Pacific Railroad vice-president Charles A. Roberts stated that he would ask the City of Westwego for a permit to demolish the ruins of the plantation house. Roberts said that he had previously asked for a permit but only got a stay of execution.

Mayor Tassin said that he had decided not to issue a demolition permit to the railroad until July 1, 1977, some two months later, even though the extension had ended. He did add, however, that if officials from the railroad requested a demolition permit, the city would be obligated to consider their request. The mayor again stressed his concerns for the safety of people who trespassed near the ruins. He further stated that neither he nor the city's Board of Aldermen were prepared to accept responsibility for accidents or injuries that might occur on the property.[24]

The mayor stated that the City of Westwego now estimated the total cost of restoring the mansion to top two million dollars, an amount that the city could not pay. The city was also financially unable to stabilize the ruins, an idea preservationists continued to encourage.

As a last effort to save the quickly dying mansion, preservationists Swanson, Christovich, McCloskey, and John Geiser created a nonprofit corporation, Seven Oaks, Inc., for the sole purpose of saving the plantation.[25] The group members sought to gain publicity to disseminate as much information as possible about the plantation and ongoing preservation efforts. They met with Westwego leaders and state officials and pleaded with the railroad, but in the end, the efforts were fruitless.[26]

A Westwego city attorney informed officials of the Texas-Pacific-Missouri-Pacific Railroad that their company was liable for the condition of the Seven Oaks mansion. At this point, the railroad estimated the cost of stabilizing the ruins at two million dollars. In response to the city attorney, it filed for a permit to demolish the ruins of the house. The railroad vice-president Charles Roberts, said, "we asked Westwego for a permit to demolish . . . unless the Mayor agrees to relieve us of responsibility . . . We need jobs a damn sight worse than we need museums. It would ruin a good industrial tract if they went in there and rebuilt it." Sadly, Roberts couldn't see what preservationists saw—Seven Oaks Plantation not only as a museum but also as a thriving economic entity. It could have been a booming tourist attraction that would have rivaled any other in the state, an attraction that would have brought a great deal of wealth to Westwego and to Jefferson Parish. It could have brought many jobs for residents—perhaps, indirectly, even more jobs than Charles Roberts and the railroad could have provided.[27]

On August 27, 1977, around 7:00 in the morning, bulldozers barged onto the site of the mansion unbeknownst to the citizens of Westwego. These machines carefully danced around the dozens of oil tanks that surrounded the house until they found their target: the old mansion. It took only a short time for the bulldozers to charge through this historic home and destroy it completely. Afterwards, men loaded some of the rubble into trucks and carried away the pieces. Railroad vice-president Charles Roberts said, "I talked to the mayor and he said it was all right . . . The job [demolition and partial clearing] took about an hour and a half."[28]

Westwego alderman Ted Munch said, "You just don't take 137 years of history and run a bulldozer through it and tote it off." Many area residents

Fig. 17. The plantation being destroyed. Even the men operating the bulldozers understood to some degree the historic importance of their actions. One man photographed the event from start to finish. Photograph courtesy of the Westwego Historical Museum and the Westwego Historical Society, Daniel P. Alario Sr., Curator and President, Westwego, Louisiana.

felt the same way. A piece of Louisiana's history had been destroyed. In an hour and a half the decades-long battle to save the ailing plantation house was over. This plantation was an institution that had been in operation longer than most any other in the Gulf South. It was born almost simultaneously with the City of New Orleans. It grew under French and Spanish colonial domination and had bloomed turbulently, yet successfully, during its passionate teenage years. It matured through young adulthood with the coming of the sugar revolution and survived the harrowing midlife crisis of the Civil War. Finally, it grew old as a resort and a private home. This great institution was now ravaged and discarded as if its life held no meaning or worth whatsoever.[29]

Mildred Stehle Harris, a former Seven Oaks resident, provided the best summary: "It makes me sad to think that a place that gave so many people happiness is just allowed to be thrown aside . . . The railroad destroyed the house, they deliberately let it fall apart."[30]

One wonders if railroad officials from another part of the country would have shared the warm feelings that so many local people had for this mansion.

Railroad officials did not see Seven Oaks as the historical treasure it was. They did not see the significance it held for the people of the state or the potential it had to become an unmatched tourist attraction. They did not see the thousands of lives that had been touched by this gem along the Mississippi River. In the end, because of what railroad officials and local leaders failed to see, a historical treasure of international importance was lost forever.

Life Among the Ruins

A great building . . . must begin with the unmeasurable, must go
through measurable means when it is being designed and
in the end must be unmeasurable.

—LOUIS KAHN, "ON ARCHITECTURE FOR ACADEMIA"

After the senseless destruction of the Seven Oaks mansion, one couple took
the opportunity to breathe new life into the old house that was no more.
By creating a dream home of their own from the rubble that remained of
the old plantation house, Dr. Henry Andressen and his wife, Kay, in their
own special way, saved the memory of Seven Oaks.

The Andressens always loved Louisiana history. Even as young sweet-
hearts, they often visited old plantations and studied their history. Kay
remembers visiting Seven Oaks before it was torn down. She and Henry
would climb through the ruins to inspect the old house and its unique
architecture. She remembers admiring the wild strawberry plants that grew
near the mansion. Each time the couple visited Seven Oaks, they observed
that something else was missing and the mansion had deteriorated a bit
more. "There was a sadness," she said, "when [we] visited that house and
realized what was happening to it."[1]

The Andressens became more involved in their study of plantations,
attempting to find a link to the past that they could own themselves. Soon
the couple discovered that link when they began purchasing antiques.
Little by little, they accumulated a substantial collection, which they
packed away in storage. As their collection grew, the Andressens decided
that they needed a home to store their accumulation of pieces of the past,
but not just any home would do; they dreamed of a home built from original old materials. They contacted architect A. Hays Town, who was world

famous for having his designs constructed with original materials taken from old structures. The Andressens were disappointed to learn that Town had a long waiting list but decided to put their names on it anyway, hoping that they would be contacted by the architect sooner rather than later.

Three years later, in August 1977, A. Hays Town finally contacted the Andressens. They told the aging architect of the plantation mansion's destruction. He instructed them to "buy everything you can get your hands on." The couple took him seriously, purchasing forty tandem truckloads of salvageable materials from the plantation site. Most of the materials that could be used were beams, bricks, and door jams. The couple salvaged the old handmade bricks, which were aged and covered with dirt. "We cleaned each one of them ourselves," Kay recalls.

Town sat down with the couple, asking them about what they wanted out of a house. He evaluated their lifestyle and meticulously formulated his design. The architect presented them with plans for a working 1795 plantation house, reminiscent of those constructed during Louisiana's Spanish dominion. Town believed that the design of an earlier house would suit the Andressens' modern-day lifestyle better than an 1830s Greek Revival-style structure like the original mansion at Seven Oaks.

When they were first presented with the design for the house, the Andressens had their doubts. They were afraid they could not afford to build such a house and that the plan was too large. "Don't ask me why," Town told the couple, "but I know that you are supposed to have this." Town instructed the couple to get started on the house exactly as he had designed it, and to leave rooms unfinished if they had to. "This house is for you," the architect said.

The Andressens took Town's advice and began work on their monumental project. Custom millwork was required to blend in old architectural pieces into the new structure. The Andressens were able to salvage the massive cypress door jams from the Seven Oaks mansion and incorporate them into their new home. The door jams, which were several inches thick and carved out of solid pieces of wood, made an impressive start to what was to be a very unique house.

The Andressens, with the help of Town, continued to acquire old building materials from various locations. The architect loved to work with old barge boards,[2] so the Andressens obtained many. They searched everywhere and, little by little, accumulated a large stash of architectural antiques. The couple obtained an old cast iron fence to install around the house, but Town told them, "We don't use everything we have." The architect wanted an original hand-hewn, split cypress fence and would accept no substitutes. The Andressens drove through the country looking for such a fence but, even after weeks of searching, were unable to find one. One day while taking a familiar route through Old Metairie, Kay decided to go a different way. The fence was the last thing on her mind. She turned onto a street and immediately saw a house adjacent to a square of land dotted with grazing horses. She could hardly believe what she saw. Surrounding the property was the perfect hand-hewn split cypress fence. To the embarrassment of her daughter, she got out of the car and knocked on the front door of the house. She introduced herself and offered not only to buy the gentlemen's fence but also to install a brand new one in its place. The gentleman then revealed that he didn't want to take down the fence because he was being paid to keep the horses. The two exchanged names and telephone numbers, but, before she left, the gentlemen asked Kay if she was related to the obstetrician, Dr. Henry Andressen. She immediately told him that the doctor was her husband. She was delighted to find out that her husband had delivered all of the man's grandchildren. The man further explained that one of his daughters had a particularly troublesome labor, and the family credited Dr. Andressen with getting her through it and saving his grandchild's life. Kay rushed home to tell her husband about her find. He telephoned the gentleman the same evening and convinced him that by selling every other board on the fence, the property would still be surrounded by adequate fence to protect his horses, and Town would have his perfect fence. Soon after, the Andressens were spending each afternoon detaching every other board from the split cypress fence in Old Metairie, loading them onto the roof of their vehicle, and transporting them to Kenner, where they were meticulously assembled into a perfect fence.

After two years of construction, the Andressens moved into their new home, even though the structure was not completely finished. It took an additional five years to complete the entire house. During this time, the most difficult task was finding people who were capable of doing this type of construction—people who had the training to use actual pieces of history in a new construction project. It was also difficult for the Andressens to move the large amounts of materials they had acquired for the construction from place to place. Storing these materials also proved to be a challenge. The Andressens rented spaces from junkyards in order to store the large beams and other such building materials until they were needed.

When asked if there was ever a point during this prolonged construction that she became discouraged or felt as if the project would never be finished, Kay answered jokingly, "It was such a gradual process . . . that each time one thing got finished, I thought [that the entire project] was complete." She remembered that on many occasions when her husband returned home from work, he would install a door casing. On one occasion, proud of his accomplishment with the casting, Henry told his wife, "There, it's finished."

"But look at how many more [door castings] you still have left to install," she jeered. Even after the construction of the house was finally complete, the project was not finished. Town wanted the house filled with original Audubon prints and, of course, the Andressens obliged. They also had to move their massive collections of antique furnishings and accessories into the house, a monumental job in itself. Before the house was even completed, it was apparent that the job of maintenance was to be enormous. Even polishing the wood in the house could not be done by standard modern means; instead, Kay had to rub the wood with beeswax, as was done hundreds of years ago, in order to maintain the historic integrity of the pieces.

The area behind and around the house provided the perfect spot for Henry's hobby of cultivating Louisiana plants. First, the architect instructed the couple on planting the seven oak trees so as not to disturb the foundation of the house. They were reminiscent of the seven oaks that once surrounded the original mansion. Then the Andressens planted seven cypress trees along the back of the property bordering the edge of Lake Pontchartrain. They also accumulated many other plants native to Louisiana and planted them among man-made waterfalls and streams running through the property. Leftover original bricks from Seven Oaks were fashioned into a fountain, and an old iron sugar kettle was turned into a lily pond. But the centerpiece of the house's grounds is a waist-high piece of an original column from Seven Oaks. It is the largest original piece of column from the plantation house known to exist. On top of this column peacefully rests a sundial. Like the house itself, the lone column stands as a relic to the South's distant past—a tranquil, glimmering gem of history. The Andressens care for the garden themselves, just as they care for every inch of their home. They have become the stewards of a historical legacy, centuries older than their own home.

After living in the house for many years, the Andressens felt it was time to share their home, which they appropriately named Seven Oaks Plantation, with others. They turned the house into a bed and breakfast. Visitors came from all over to enjoy a night or two in this modern, yet historical, house. Today, a passerby driving down Gay Lynn Drive in the modern, affluent neighborhood bordering Lake Pontchartrain can find Henry Andressen outside amid the waterfalls and streams, tending to his prized plants and botanicals, and Kay Andressen inside cleaning the centuries-old doorframes with beeswax or in the kitchen preparing a plantation breakfast, just as it was done two hundred years ago.

CHAPTER TWELVE

Future of the Past

This narrow isthmus 'twixt two boundless seas,
The past, the future,—two eternities!

—THOMAS MOORE, *Lalla Rookh. The Veiled Prophet of Khorassan*

Time past and time future
What might have been and what has been
Point to one end, which is always present.

—T. S. ELIOT, *Four Quartets,* "BURNT NORTON," PT. I

Dr. Henry and Kay Andressen helped save the memory of the demolished Seven Oaks mansion, preserving what few materials were salvageable from this historic treasure. In many ways their action was a representation of what was happening throughout the South, as a new generation struggled with what to do with the vestiges of its past. Certainly, Seven Oaks and plantations like it represent a faded era—a time of southern success that was fueled by the forced labor of enslaved individuals. These dying mansions and our interaction with them are symbolic in many ways of our own internal struggle with assimilating the South's past with the South's future.

Certainly, many today would argue that the vestiges of slavery should go the way of slavery itself, but African-American opposition was never an issue in the battle for the preservation of Seven Oaks. In fact, the local African-American community members identified with the house, as many descended from the talented slaves who made the physical, social, and economic structure of the plantation a reality. Without plantations like Seven Oaks there would be little tangible evidence of slavery's existence. The plantation represented not only the planters who controlled such estates but also those whose labor fueled them. If for nothing more, Seven Oaks and the many plantations across the South should be preserved in order to memorialize those whose enslavement created the society in which such properties flourished and to provide physical evidence for successive generations of the culture and time in which man was held as property. These mansions are not crumbling old structures; they are in many ways the history of the Old South.

Seven Oaks was much more than just an old estate; it had served as a working settlement and later a plantation before the birth of George Washington, long before the American Revolution, and throughout the period of the Civil War. Founded in 1719 by the French Minister of State, who used the settlement as a depot, Seven Oaks was one of the oldest continually operating plantations in Louisiana and quite possibly the entire Gulf South. The plantation house and its occupants had seen the abolition of slavery, reconstruction, and two world wars. It had seen the flags change over Louisiana—from French to Spanish to French to American to Confederate to American again. The plantation had been a depot for enslaved human beings, a home for wealthy planters, an encampment for Confederate soldiers and later Union troops, a barracks for rowdy World War I troops, a resort for locals and tourists alike, a home for many, and, finally, a magnificent crumbling gem. Countless people were born on the site of the great plantation; many people lived there, loved there, cried there, and died there. A great tragedy occurred as this important historical treasure was ripped from the people of Louisiana against their wishes.

Never again will children see the great mansion called Seven Oaks. Today we see the huge round storage tanks that have sprouted up around the site of the mansion. An uninformed passerby would never know that this site once held one of the earliest and likely most historically significant plantations the Gulf South has ever known.

Some might say the plantation mansion should have gone, as it represented a bygone era in which human beings were held as property, but as much as Seven Oaks represented the memory of the wealthy planters and aristocrats who owned it, it also represented the slaves whose toil created the wealth that allowed such a structure to be built. It was the slaves who constructed the mansion, molding bricks for the structure with their bare hands. The structure provided physical evidence of their labor and talents.

The mansion represented the entire plantation (slaves and all) and the history of Louisiana and the South. We must not turn our back on any aspect of history; instead we must embrace it and learn from it.

The story of Seven Oaks must be a lesson for all. Never again must we allow a historical treasure to waste away. Never again must we allow a piece of our nation's heritage to be stolen away from us. By analyzing and understanding why the preservation of Seven Oaks plantation failed, we may gain important insight into social and political intricacies of southern culture and life.

We may also learn important lessons from the saga of Seven Oaks that may be useful in future preservation efforts. A number of endangered plantation mansions exist in Louisiana and throughout the South. For example, Lebeau House in St. Bernard Parish, Louisiana, is an extremely significant and historic mansion that has been neglected for years by its industrial owners. Today, a group of preservationists are fighting for restoration, but some naïve elected officials seem to be catering to whims of big business rather than the wishes of those citizens who elected them.[1]

Lebeau House is one example of many endangered plantation mansions. If nothing else, the story of Seven Oaks illustrates what can happen to a community when it allows industry to destroy its physical heritage; today tourist-friendly Westwego laments the destruction of its "main attraction." But, despite the mansion's appeal and local popularity, its remembrance has never been memorialized in physical form.

For more than twenty-five years, not even a plaque mentioning the plantation site's past or a small monument in remembrance of the many slaves and soldiers who served there has even been placed on the historic site. Fortunately, this situation is being remedied. Recently, the Jefferson Parish Historical Commission sponsored a highway marker to note the significance of the site. Following suit, the Westwego Historical Society sponsored a bronze plaque for the site. Additionally, former Jefferson Parish councilman Lloyd F. Giardina (whose ancestors once resided on the plantation) designated twenty-five thousand dollars from his district's discretionary funds for a granite monument. The historic site's new owner, Kinder-Morgan, now has an opportunity to show the people of Louisiana and the entire country that it has much more understanding, foresight, and community pride than the previous owners of the property by donating a small portion of the land for these important monuments.

Although Seven Oaks is lost, never to return, the glorious old plantation still has stories to tell. Never has a true archaeological excavation been performed on the site of the once great plantation. Many people have accidentally discovered articles throughout the years near the plantation: the farmers, who leased part of the land from the railroad, unearthed swords, and, during the construction of a petroleum storage tank, workers found six human skeletons buried in the soil. There must be thousands more artifacts waiting to be unearthed and to unleash their secrets.

Surely the area on which the house and other structures (huts, slave cabins, kitchens, shops, mills, warehouses, depots, the canal) stood, along with surrounding lands, will provide amazing artifacts and unprecedented knowledge about the workings of both a pre- and a post-Civil War plantation. In fact, a brief, informal, preliminary survey of this historic site by a Louisiana archaeologist resulted in quite promising findings: without even touching the dirt, the scholar identified small artifacts (including a small but very fine piece of antebellum china) simply lying on the soil. If such artifacts are literally lying on the ground, the richness of what lies beneath must be even more significant. It is important that such excavations begin now before artifacts are further disturbed, damaged, or totally destroyed.

Furthermore, the plantation's early use as a slave depot makes such an archaeological undertaking vastly more important. The site of very few such depots can be accurately determined, and the Seven Oaks site's remarkable preservation (the site is fenced in and the underlying ground has been virtually untouched with the exception of the tanks that are located on some of the property) may make it one of the most important archaeological sites relating to early slavery in the United States. Archaeological study is needed now.

Archaeology is the future of Seven Oaks because destruction was its past. Despite the valiant efforts of dozens of concerned citizens and public officials, this plantation was allowed to be demolished by the Texas-Pacific-Missouri-Pacific Railroad and its indifferent attitude. We must work to right this wrong by persuading the current owners and lessees of the site to allow archeological excavation of the entire plantation. Louisiana's universities certainly have fine anthropology departments, made up of many celebrated archaeologists who would be capable of undertaking this important scientific and historical expedition. Furthermore, Louisiana boasts progressive regional archaeological programs that regularly undertake excavation projects, and the leaders of these programs have expressed great interest in the site.

Archaeological treasures and knowledge uncovered through excavation would make impressive additions to Westwego's newly formed historic district, located on Sala Avenue in the original Salaville community, near the site of the mansion and originally part of the plantation grounds. Many locals still possess pieces of the plantation that they gathered one way or another. These pieces could be displayed for all to enjoy. Old photographs, paintings, and drawings of Seven Oaks could be taken from dark closets and attics and put on display for the world to see.

This centerpiece of archaeological and historical wealth, if maintained in an educational and public venture such as a local museum, would provide the people of America and the entire world with an unequaled look into the lives of area planters and the early history of Louisiana. It also would provide indirect success to local business; calculable tax revenue to local, parish, and state governments; an unsurpassed tourist attraction for the west bank; and many needed jobs for area residents.

Some have even suggested reconstructing the plantation, a task that would be difficult but by no means impossible. The complete and accurate reconstruction of a lost antebellum plantation mansion is an undertaking that has already successfully been completed in Louisiana. Greenwood Plantation in St. Francisville burned to the ground but has since been totally reconstructed and now serves as a very successful tourist attraction, bed and breakfast location, and wedding venue. It serves not only to entertain but also to memorialize the people of the past, to interpret life on the antebellum plantation, and to provide an educational venue where tourists from around the world can learn and experience the South's complex past. In addition, Greenwood serves an important economic function—attracting tourists and visitors and bringing in jobs and revenue for the local community and surrounding areas.

If the mansion is reconstructed, so should be the remainder of the plantation, including the slave cabins, sugar house, barns, and outbuildings. Any reconstruction should certainly tell the entire story of the plantation, not just that of the rich white owners. In their book, *Representations of Slavery*, Jennifer L. Eichstedt and Stephen Small analyzed their tours of 122 plantation museums mostly in Louisiana, Virginia, and Georgia.

They found that only a few (including Louisiana's own Laura Plantation, which burned in 2004) dealt with the issue of slavery in a straightforward, educational manner. Most trivialized the issue or simply did not mention it at all, "symbolically annihilating" this critically significant part of American history and the history of the sites themselves. Others only included accept-able mentions of slaves in special tours designed to appeal to African-American visitors. A reconstruction of Seven Oaks plantation could fill this void in the plantation museum industry by setting a standard of not only adequately addressing the issue of slavery but presenting the entire planta-tion operation and its many social, political, and economic intricacies in an educational, truthful, and interesting manner for all visitors.[2]

While reconstructing Seven Oaks and interpreting the site in a realistic, educational manner may be difficult, there exists a great textual and photo-graphic record of the plantation (in the Historic American Building Survey, or HABS, and other collections) to aid in the task. In addition, thanks to architect Davis Jahncke, detailed and accurate plans for the house are read-ily available. Period maps (many published in this volume) also provide diagrams for reconstructing an accurate layout of slave cabins and other buildings. The existing records and accounts of the house would provide plenty of information and physical evidence for an exact reconstruction.

If Seven Oaks Plantation were reconstructed, it would be the closest such plantation to the City of New Orleans and could be easily accessed from the nearby Huey P. Long Bridge (which is set to be widened providing an even greater transportation route) or from the new Lazy River Landing that trav-erses the Mississippi at Westwego. The attraction would also be easily acces-sible to the Crescent City Connection via the West Bank Expressway. Because of these facts, Seven Oaks would surely be the most successful of all the great plantation homes that are open to the public. Such a venue would not only complement Westwego's efforts to promote its historical treasures as tourist attractions but would also serve as the crowning jewel of Westwego's historic revitalization efforts, bringing vast numbers of people into the city and into the Salaville Historic District. It would provide an unparalleled opportunity to educate people from all corners of the globe about the Old South and its rich, intricate heritage. Furthermore, a reconstruction of Seven Oaks plantation would spearhead a remarkable economic boom for the City of Westwego and the west bank region of the greater New Orleans area.

It has been estimated that a completely reconstructed Seven Oaks on its original site (along with educational tours, a wedding service, overnight accommodations, restaurant facilities, a gift shop, and all the amenities of other publicly accessible plantation mansions) may have up to a $100 million annual economic impact on the local area. And it is important to remember that when the plantation served a similar function in the late nineteenth century; it was met with unprecedented success.

A Tulane University scholar, Dr. Chizuko Izawa, who has outlined an economic development plan for the area focused around the reconstruction of Seven Oaks, agrees that reconstructing the plantation should be a top economic priority for the region. She wrote,

> It is now up to all the people of Westwego to rise to the occasion of honoring that proud symbol of their ancestors' labors by promptly planning for its early reconstruction . . . The project is not only designed to revive Westwego's colorful historic heritage of its people, but also to engender a major economic expansion, in short to provide a stimulus package to insure the city's prosperity far into the future, something far greater than the Westwego region has ever seen. It is an investment adventure destined to succeed. History tells us that the plantation and its gardens attracted 10,000–20,000 visitors, coming in ferry boats in a single day [Columbia Gardens, see chapter 7]: The entrance fees of $5 to the mansion and gardens alone will generate $50,000 to $100,000 a day! Imagine how many more dollars visitors are likely to leave in Westwego via purchases of food, beverages and souvenirs. With easy access via the Huey P. Long Bridge or from the new ferry from the East Bank, daily visitors today would far exceed earlier figures above, many times over.
>
> By rebuilding Seven Oaks, the region's crown jewel, Westwego has the opportunity to become another exemplary town by teaching the world that reverence for history needs not be divorced from sound and profitable business ventures. I believe firmly that the investments now required to develop Seven Oaks would bring with them unprecedented economic expansion and much renewed pride in the City.[3]

Although reconstruction may be in the distant future for Seven Oaks, it is vastly important that the plantation site be properly physically identified with a commemorative marker immediately. The area should also be set aside as an official historic site, and national register status should be sought in order to preserve the property. After this, archaeological study should commence. If the local community and larger regional public sees fit, the possibilities for funding a complete reconstruction should be further investigated and wider resources should be identified. A public committee or private foundation, or both, should be established to work toward this ultimate attainable goal.

What happens to the site of Seven Oaks in the future will surely be symbolic of the community's sentiment toward its ambivalent legacy and characteristic of the power and politics of the time. Perhaps the community will eventually unite and change this story's unhappy ending to one of rediscovery and rebirth, thereby adding another chapter to the history of Seven Oaks.

Appendix I

*Chronological Chain of Title and Timeline of Major Events
in the History of the Plantation Known as Seven Oaks*

The following chain of title was abstracted from public records from both the Notarial Archives in New Orleans and the Jefferson Parish Courthouse in Gretna, Louisiana. Information was also adapted from the Historic American Buildings Survey report by Samuel Wilson Jr. and the *Louisiana Historical Quarterly* and a variety of other historical accounts and sources.

It is interesting to note that several sources cite wealthy planter Lucian LaBranche and his family as owning Seven Oaks Plantation. However, the chain of title clearly shows that LaBranche never owned the plantation. Perhaps it was an error from one source that was carried to others, or perhaps the LaBranche family occupied the home after the death of Camille Zeringue but never actually owned the house. One of the earliest sources that mentions the LaBranche family's connection to Seven Oaks is a book by William P. Spratling and Natalie Scott, *Old Plantation Houses in Louisiana*, published in 1927. It seems that this error was include in a book by Dr. Herman de Bachelle Seebold, *Old Louisiana Plantation Homes and Family Trees*, and then in several other sources.

Period maps show the LaBranche family owning property near the Zeringue plantation, definitely making them neighbors. However, no evidence has surfaced that places the LaBranches at Seven Oaks.

1718   Jean Baptiste Le Moyne, sieur de Bienville, founds Nouvelle Orléans.

1719   First slave ships arrive in the French colony of Louisiana. November 18: The Company of the Indies grants a concession to the French Minister of State, Monsieur LeBlanc, and three of his associates: the Marquis d'Asfeld, Marshal of France and Director General of Fortifications; the Compte de Belle Isle, Lieutenant-General of the King's Armies; and Gerard Michel de la Jonchere, Treasurer General of the Military Order of St. Louis. These distinguished French gentlemen raised among themselves a total sum of 400,000 livres for this concession, which included Petit Desert, land below New Orleans on the west bank known as Chaouachas, and additional land at Natchez.

1720   Johann Michael Zerhinger (Zeringue) arrives in New Orleans with his wife, Ursula Spaet, and daughter Marie Salome. June 30: The first people who settled the Petit Desert area set sail from the Port of L'Orient in France under the command of Captain Ignace Francois Broutin.

1722   The capital of Louisiana moves from Old Biloxi to New Orleans.

1724   Johann Michael Zerhinger seeks to leave the Colony but is persuaded to stay and continue his work on the parish church.

1726   September 18: Michael Zerhinger's daughter, Marie Salome, dies. November 1: Michael Zerhinger's wife, Ursula Spaet, dies. December 26: Michael Zerhinger weds Barbara Haertel, the widow of Mangus Albert and Joseph Ballif.

1732   Future president George Washington is born in Westmoreland County, Virginia.

1737   Michael Zerhinger and wife, Barbara Heartel, have a son, Jean-Louis.

1738   January 28: The LeBlanc Concessions, including Petit Desert, sold by the original owners, the French Minister of State LeBlanc and his associates, to Sieurs Joseph Assailly and Charles Favre Daunoy. Records describe the Petit Desert property at this time as "fourteen arpents of land frontage by the ordinary depth, situated at the place called the 'Little Desert', about 1 league above New Orleans on the other side of the river, with the huts, appurtenances and dependencies thereon."

1752   March 6: Charles Favre Daunoy acquires Joseph Assailly's interest in the plantation by a transaction at Cap Francois.

1759   January 4: Claude Joseph Villars Dubreuil Jr. purchases Petit Desert Plantation from the widow of Charles Favre Daunoy, Catherine Hubert Bellair.

1761   Claude Joseph Dubreuil Jr. "complained that wild horses from the herd of Jean Baptiste Massey, established along Bayou des Familles in 1726, were invading havoc."[1]

1762   June 6: Jean Louis Zeringue marries Marie Francois Hubert LaCroix, the daughter of Daniel Rene Bellaire LaCroix and Marie Catherine Henry. The couple has eleven children, including Michael Zeringue, who later purchases Petit Desert from his father-in-law, Alexandre Harang. November: By the Treaty of Fontainebleau, Spain gains control of all of the Louisiana Colony west of the Mississippi River (including Petit Desert) and the "Isle of Orleans" (New Orleans) on the east bank of the river.

1768 February 1: Sheriff Joseph Maison is ordered to seize the property of Claude Joseph Villars Dubreuil Jr. October 5: Governor Unzaga orders the property of Claude Joseph Villars Dubreuil Jr. to be seized in order to recover what was owed to his creditors.

1772 Pedro Delille Dupart acquires the plantation at an auction of the property of Claude Joseph Villars Dubreuil Jr. Francisco Bouligny also acquires a portion of the plantation at the same auction.

1773 June 14: Francisco Bouligny states he purchased the plantation called "Barataria" at auction in the previous year.

1775 March 27: Pedro Delille Dupart sells the Petit Desert plantation to Jean Louis Trudeau.

1785 November 21: Alexandre Harang buys 12 arpents from Jean Louis Trudeau.

1787 May 25-September 17: The United States drafts the Constitution in Philadelphia.

1788 November 11: Michel Zeringue, son of Jean Louis Zeringue and Marie Francois Hubert LaCroix (and grandson of Johann Michael Zerhinger), marries Marie Josephe Harang.

c. 1790 Camille Zeringue born to Michel Zeringue and Marie Josephe Harang.

1794 January 31: Alexandre Harang sells 10 arpents of land to his son-in-law, Michel Zeringue, "with all the buildings which are constructed on it, their implements, utensils, groves and fences . . . with the expressed condition that Mousieur Lebreton shall enjoy the canal which passes by said land while he is a neighbor."

1800 October: Spain cedes Louisiana to France in the Treaty of San Ildefonso.

1803 April 30: Napoleon agrees to sell Louisiana to the United States. This, the largest real estate transaction in history, comes to be known as the "Louisiana Purchase."

1811	March 10: Michel Zeringue leaves his plantation to his wife, Marie Josephe Harang, and his children.
1812	Louisiana enters the Union as the eighteenth state. The United States confirms Zeringue is in possession of 34 arpents of land.
1815	November 28: Marie Josephe Harang, the widow of Michel Zeringue, donates 8 arpents of land to her son, Camille Zeringue.
1822	March 28: Camille Zeringue acquires a parcel of land (Section or lot 29 T 135 – R. 23 E) from the United States.
1825	February 11: The Louisiana Legislature officially creates Jefferson Parish. March 5: Michel Zeringue's daughter, Marie Azelie Zeringue, sells property described as "one undivided half of each, a plantation situated on the right bank of the river, at a distance of about two and one half leagues above New Orleans, having eight arpents frontage by 100 in depth, bounded on one side by the property of Louis Cesar Le Breton Deschapelles, and on the other by that of the said Camille Zeringue, including all buildings and appurtances, acquired by Mrs. Lombard as a donation from the late Michael Zeringue and Mrs. Josephine, alias Josette Harang, her father and mother by act before Narcisse Broutin, July 13, 1813."[2]
1826	May 31: Camille Zeringue inherits 3 arpents from the succession of F. Zeringue.
1827	June 6: Camille Zeringue marries Madelein Lise Roman, the daughter of Onisime Roman and Celeste Cantrelle.
1829	Camille Zeringue helps organize the Barataria and Lafourche Canal Company.
1830	January 13: Camille Zeringue obtains 3 arpents from the succession of his brother Jean Fortuné Zeringue. April 21: Camille Zeringue sells land and the canal to the Barataria Canal Corporation.
c. 1840	Zeringues complete construction of Greek Revival columned mansion.
1844	Norbert Rillieux, a free man of color, invents a machine that refines sugar by recycling steam from vacuum pans. This process increases sugar production efficiency.

1848   April 4: Camille Zeringue inherits 12 arpents from the succession of his mother, the widow of Michel Zeringue. Camille Zeringue buys additional land from his sister, Azelie.

1852   October 14: Camille Zeringue grants the right-of-way through his plantation to the New Orleans, Opelousas, and Great Western Railroad with the condition that no station be placed on his property.

1854   December 7: Camille Zeringue acquires a parcel of land (Section or lot 35 T. 135 – R. 23 E) from the state of Louisiana to expand his holdings.

1861   January 23: Louisiana holds a state convention concerning the possibility of secession. January 26: A Louisiana state convention passes an ordinance of secession from the Union without submitting it for popular vote.

1862   May: Confederates at Algiers seize a railroad engine from federal control, ride to Jefferson Station near the Zeringue plantation, and begin to destroy the tracks in order to limit Union transportation capabilities.

1863   October 12: Jean Fortuné Zeringue enlists as a Confederate private at Mobile, Alabama, joining Company F of the 30th Louisiana Infantry. His two brothers also fight for the Confederate cause.

1866   Authorities seize and auction much of Camille Zeringue's property, including "cane knives (used in harvesting sugar cane), a cotton gin and cotton press, a corn mill, a mowing machine, 32 stacks of rice in sacks, 200 barrels of threshed rice in sacks, a saw mill, hogs, cows, a bull, mules, oxen, chickens and pigeons, horses, plows, carts and tools."[3]

1867   General Philip Henry Sheridan takes control of Louisiana; it becomes part of the Fifth Military District.

1870   May: The railroad brings Camille Zeringue to court seeking to expropriate the plantation's land and river front in order to build wharves and terminals; courts allow expropriation.

1872   January 6: Camille Zeringue dies at age 82 at his plantation. The funeral is held the next day at St. Mary's Assumption Church in New Orleans with burial at the St. Louis Cemetery.

1891	November 16: The Citizen's Bank of Louisiana forecloses on the widow and heirs of Camille Zeringue by sheriff's deed. In total, 34 arpents are seized.
1892	March 7: Pablo Sala acquires the plantation from the Citizen's Bank of Louisiana. The plantation is transformed into Columbia Gardens Pleasure Resort.
1893	July 4: Columbia Gardens hosts one of its biggest events, an Independence Day celebration attended by 20,000 guests, each paying fifteen cents that covers both round-trip ferry service and admission to the resort.
1894	October: Pablo Sala dies.
1895	April 16: Pablo Sala's sister, Maria Sala y Fabregas, inherits the plantation.
1898	February 11: After Maria Sala y Fabregas's death, ownership of the plantation passes to Narcisso Barres Durell.
1901	September 21: Narcisso Barres Durell transfers ownership of the plantation to Alphonse A. Lelong.
1902	September 10: Alphonse A. Lelong transfers ownership of the plantation to his company, the A. A. Lelong Land and Improvement Association, Ltd.
1906	May: Charles T. Soniat acquires the plantation from the A. A. Lelong Land and Improvement Association, Ltd.
1912	April 24: Charles T. Soniat sells the plantation to E. G. Merriam, a trustee of the Missouri-Pacific Railroad Company.
1917	April 6: The United States declares war on Germany, officially entering World War I. The plantation is soon used as a barracks for soldiers.
1918	August 12: A detachment of enlisted men, Company "D" 4th Battalion U.S. Guards under the command of 2nd Lieutenant Theodore H. Martin, leaves Camp Nicholls, Louisiana, to take station at Westwego,

relieving Det. 43rd Infantry, guarding the railroad, wharves, and grain elevators. November 11: The signing of the armistice ends World War I.

1919   The Stehle Family moves into Seven Oaks.

1927   A great storm floods the Mississippi River, which threatens to lap over the levee. William Howard Stehle spends the night supervising sand-bagging on the levee, while his horrified family waits in the mansion. The levee holds.

1954   The Stehles vacate Seven Oaks due to a large leak in the roof.

1955   The mansion begins to fade; over time vagrants, vandals, and treasure hunters would contribute to the decline of the mansion.

1957   Preservationists prompt the American Liberty Oil Company (who sublease the site of the plantation from the Missouri-Pacific Railroad) to do something to preserve the structure. The oil company, led by President James J. Coleman, invests $3,000 on a new temporary roof for the old mansion. The oil company also cleans up the grounds surrounding the mansion, stabilizes the structure, and builds a shell-lined drive from the road to the house. Both the Louisiana Landmarks Society and the American Liberty Oil Company sponsor public opening of the mansion. April 14: The Louisiana Landmarks Society sponsors a "Fête Champetre" to raise funds to restore the house.

1965   Hurricane Betsy ravages southeastern Louisiana and the Gulf Coast. The belvedere at Seven Oaks is destroyed, and the roof is badly damaged. The mansion continues to fade.

1973   Truman Capote visits the Seven Oaks mansion for a photo shoot.

1975   November: A Westwego city attorney orders the Missouri-Pacific-Texas-Pacific Railroad to repair the crumbling Seven Oaks mansion or demolish it.

1976   February: The Westwego Board of Aldermen condemns the ruined mansion and orders it to be demolished.

1977   August 27: The Missouri-Pacific-Texas-Pacific Railroad demolishes Seven Oaks Plantation Mansion.

1980s	Dr. and Mrs. Henry Andressen construct their home using some original materials, obtained from the ruins at Seven Oaks.
1996	Lifelong Westwego residents Daniel P. Alario Sr. and Zenobia "Bebe" Rebstock Alario publish *Westwego from Cheniere to Canal,* the first of several Westwego history books. The book is met with great anticipation and ignites interest in the city's past.
1997	Daniel P. Alario Sr. incorporates the Westwego Historical Society, fostering interest and research in the history of the area.
2002	The twenty-fifth anniversary of the demolition of the house is remembered in a variety of ways, including a special presentation at an annual banquet in honor of the founding of Jefferson Parish. Jefferson Historical Society of Louisiana publishes "Seven Oaks Plantation: A Lasting Legacy" by Marc Matrana in *Jefferson History Notebook,* vol. 6, no. 1. The plantation property is sold by the Union Pacific Railroad to Kinder-Morgan, Inc.
2003	The Westwego Historical Society, the Jefferson Parish Historical Commission, and Jefferson Parish councilman Lloyd F. Giardina provides funds for commemorative plaques and a marble monument for the site of Seven Oaks.
2004–2005	Negotiations to allow a small portion of the plantation property for the erection of commemorative plaques and the development of a small roadside monument park continue.

APPENDIX II

Slaves Owned by Camille Zeringue,
as listed in the 1860 United States Census Slave Schedules

Males

Ages: 76, 75, 67, 66, 66, 64, 64, 60, 58, 58, 58, 58, 58, 58, 56, 50, 50, 49, 48, 48, 48, 48, 46, 46, 44, 44, 43, 40, 40, 40, 40, 38, 36, 36, 35, 35, 35, 30, 28, 28, 28, 28, 28, 28, 26, 26, 26, 20, 20, 20, 20, 20, 20, 20, 18, 18, 18, 18, 18, 18, 18, 16, 16, 16, 16, 16, 16, 10, 10, 8

TOTAL NUMBER OF MALES: 70

Females

Ages: 65, 65, 60, 60, 58, 58, 56, 56, 55, 50, 58, 48, 48, 48, 40, 40, 36, 35, 30, 28, 28, 28, 26, 25, 8, 6, 4, 4, 4, 3, 3, 2, 1, 1, 1, 1, 1, 1

TOTAL NUMBER OF FEMALES: 38

TOTAL NUMBER OF SLAVES: 108

Note: Unfortunately, names were not given in this reference for the Zeringue slaves.

APPENDIX III

Comparative Data of the Largest Slaveholders in Jefferson Parish

A "large slaveholder" in Louisiana was defined as a man who owned fifty or more slaves. The following is a comparative list of those in Jefferson Parish who met this definition in 1860. The raw data was collected from federal census records and the book *The Large Slaveholders of Louisiana—1860* by Joseph Karl Menn. Statistical data were computed by Marc R. Matrana.

Name	Age	# of slaves	sugar (1000 lbs)	Molasses (Gallons)
Berthoud, M.	–	155	650	42,000
Bolb, C. P. & W.	46 / 52	149	–	–
Cagnolatti, A. & P.	45 / 34	52	325	–
Drouet, J. B. & Ed	66 / 70	120	450	35,000
Dugue, F.	45	81	–	–
Dusseau, Charles	52	108	400	24,000
Eganey Estate	–	144	–	–
Hodge Plantation	–	150	–	–
Fortier, P.	33	50	–	–
Gardere & Labarre	–	65	–	–
Gardere and Lous	68	59	–	–
Harvey, P. A.	–	51	–	–
Johnson & Gossett	52 / 40	60	200	20,000
Labarre, A. B.	35	56	65	11,000
Labranche, B.	40	160	650	42,000
Marshall, L. R.	70	91	350	22,000
Mason, W. F.	46	83	400	32,000
Millaudon, H. C.	35	440	1,000	93,000
Osborne, H.	–	57	600	32,000
Pritchard, Dr.	–	55	–	–
Rosse, Widow	–	63	–	–
Saul, Thomas	56	96	330	25,000
Sauve, Pierre	55	109	400	32,000
Soniat, Theodore	37	145	600	60,000

Name	Age	# of slaves	sugar (1000 lbs)	Molasses (Gallons)
Sparks, D. P.	70	123	400	3,200
Vicknair, M.	–	56	–	–
Waggaman, Widow	66	160	500	30,000
Zeringue, Camille	68	107	300	18,000
Unknown	–	55	–	–

Large Slaveholders of Jefferson Parish
1860 Farm Statistics

	Average across large slaveholders	Median across large slaveholders	Camille Zeringue
Number of horses owned	11	10	20
Number of milch cows owned	12.3	12	20
Bushels of Indian corn* produced	4,105	4,000	7,800
Bushels of Irish potatoes* produced	263	150	150

*Of those producing and reporting this crop.
Note: Numbers have been rounded where appropriate.

Large Slaveholders of Jefferson Parish
1860 Slave Statistics

	Average across large slaveholders	Median across large slaveholders	Camille Zeringue
Number of slaves owned	107	91*	107**
Number of slave dwellings	21	20	23
Number of slaves per dwelling	5.05	5.00	4.65

*In this case the average is somewhat skewed due to one slaveholder with an unusually large number of slaves (H. C. Millaudon with 440 slaves); therefore, the median is the more robust figure.
**A discrepancy of one slave exists between this value and that presented earlier from the census. This could be the result of a slight error in one of the sources, but it is more likely due to the birth, death, sale, or purchase of one slave.

Total number of slaves held by the large slaveholders in Jefferson Parish: 3,100
Note: Numbers have been rounded where appropriate.

Large Slaveholders of Jefferson Parish
1860 Economic Statistics

	Average across large slaveholders	Median across large slaveholders	Camille Zeringue
Cash value of farm	$101,894.74*	$80,000	$90,000
Number of acres of improved land owned	786	650	600
Value of real property	$114,500	$85,000	$90,000
Value of farm implements	$1,836.25	$1,250	$1,500

*In this table, the average is somewhat skewed due to one slaveholder with an unusually large, high-valued farm (H. C. Millaudon with a farm worth $500,000); therefore, the median is the more robust figure. For more information about the Millaudon Plantation see Marc R. Matrana, "On Cane and Coolies: Chinese Laborers on Post-Antebellum Louisiana Sugar Plantations As Exemplified on the Millaudon Plantation of Jefferson Parish." Jefferson History Notebook. Vol. 7, No. 1. February 2003.

Note: Numbers have been rounded where appropriate.

APPENDIX IV

Brief Historical Sketch of Zeringue Family in Louisiana

Michel Zeringue, who purchased the plantation known as Petit Desert from his father-in-law, Alexandre Harang, in 1794, was the grandson of Johann Michael Zerhinger. Many sources speculate that Zerhinger, known commonly as Michael, originally came from Franconia, Bavaria, an area in present-day Germany. Some sources do question this, but it is clear that Zerhinger did speak German, so if he did not originate from Franconia, he was probably born somewhere near the region.[1]

Zerhinger was born about 1684. In 1705, he married (probably in Switzerland) Anna Maria Molerin, a native of Basil, Switzerland.[2] Anna bore Michael two daughters. The couple baptized their first daughter, Anna Maria, on January 13, 1706, in Village Neuf, Haut-Rhin, France. The child died less than four months later. A second daughter, Marie Salome, was born in 1707 and was baptized on June 29. Zerhinger's wife, Anna, died in 1711 and was buried on March 2 in Huningue, Haut-Rhin, France.[3] Less than three months later, Zerhinger wed his second wife, Ursule Spate, a native of Pejuille, Switzerland. A child was born to the couple in 1712. The couple named the baby Marguerith and baptized her on March 14, 1712. This child may have died young because she did not accompany her parents on their journey to North America.[4]

While working in France, Zerhinger was exposed to the prolific advertising campaign of businessman John Law, who promoted Louisiana in hopes of enticing people to settle in the colony. Law went to France after fleeing Scotland because he killed a man in a duel. Always looking to make a profit, Law went to great efforts to associate with the rich and powerful. One such influential aristocrat whom Law managed to charm was the Duke of Orleans, who was at the time Regent of France, as King Louis XV was too young to take control of his empire. Law approached the duke with a business venture concocted to turn the stagnant colony of Louisiana into a source of wealth for France. With France consumed with financial need, the duke agreed to the venture and granted Law a twenty-five-year monopoly in Louisiana. Law formed the Company of the West to oversee the colony. He sold stock in the company, a commodity the French purchased with great enthusiasm. The Company was required to send six thousand white settlers and three thousand slaves to the colony annually. In order to meet the quota, Law and his Company undertook a massive advertising campaign in which a multitude of circulars, handbills, and posters, among other things, were used to promote Louisiana as the "land of milk and honey." The people of Europe who witnessed this campaign pictured the unsettled Louisiana colony as a tropical paradise, often having no other information on which to base their views.

Zerhinger, along with many other Europeans, sought to leave his familiar surroundings to travel to the heavily promoted colony. Zerhinger was contracted by Law's Company, which enticed skilled laborers to come to Louisiana by offering them monetary gratuities and by paying the passage for their wives and children to go to the colony. Colonial documents suggest that it was Mr. de Boispinel, a brother of Lablond de La Tour, who approached Zerhinger and convinced him to travel to the colony. Zerhinger and his family went to the Louisiana Colony for the first time aboard *Le Dromadaire*, a ship commanded by M. de St. Marc. Zerhinger's signature, in German script, appeared on *Le Dromadaire's* passenger list. The ship, which set sail from Huningue, France, in August or September 1720, contained 150 passengers whose descendants settled in Louisiana on what is now known as the "German Coast." The ship arrived in Biloxi (in present-day Mississippi), then the capital of French Louisiana, on December 14, 1720.[5]

Upon their arrival, the Zerhingers were surprised to find that Louisiana was not the tropical paradise that they had expected but rather an undeveloped, swampy wilderness. They found limitless swamplands and marshlands plagued by infestations of rats, snakes, mosquitoes, and alligators. The primitive establishments were also regularly sieged various diseases, floods, plagues, hurricanes, and Indian raids. Despite the harsh conditions, the population of Louisiana continued to grow. In 1721, the colony had a population of 5,000.

Zerhinger found much work as a carpenter in the quickly growing colony. A report by Mr. de Boispinel dated August 18, 1722, described an incident in which Zerhinger uncovered iron wares and axes while demolishing a house belonging to a Mr. St. Martin. It was revealed that those items had been stolen, apparently by St. Martin, from a Mr. de Valdeterre. Scholars agree that the items were probably associated with the transfer of the capital from Biloxi to New Orleans, because those same types of items were mentioned as being stolen from the old fort at that time.[6]

Zerhinger, his wife, Ursula, and his daughter, Marie Salome Zehringer, made their way to New Orleans. At this time, New Orleans was little more than a village of crude dwellings made of palmettos, reeds, bark, and mud. The village had been devastated only one year earlier when a fierce hurricane caused great damage. In 1722, a second hurricane nearly destroyed the settlement.

In 1722, Zerhinger was listed as a Company of the Indies (formerly Company of the West) employee, working in New Orleans, with a salary of 400 livres annually. The French engineer, Adrien de Pauger, reported on February 9, 1724, that work on the new parish church was "unceasing." He added that the council had approved a signed contract with carpenter Zerhinger, who was already acquiring wood for the project.[7]

Officials listed Zerhinger, now also known as Michael Seringue, as the master carpenter of the first St. Louis Church on Chartres Street in New Orleans, now the present site of the Basilica, the Cathedral of St. Louis, King of France (best known as the St. Louis Cathedral) on Jackson Square. Zerhinger employed the building techniques he learned in France, but because stones were not available in the region, the area's abundant clay had to be molded into bricks. The newly established brickyard on Bayou Road provided bricks for the foundation of the church and for the filling between the heavy framing timbers on the building. This allowed de Pauger, the designer, to omit the exterior wooden buttresses he indicated on the original design. This method, called "brick between post" (briqueté entre poteaux), soon became common in the colony and continued to be used into the middle of the nineteenth century. This church may have been the first building in Louisiana to use this construction technique.[8]

In 1724, Zerhinger became frustrated with the engineers and disappointed with the pay he received for his work on the church. Consequently, he petitioned the Superior Council on December 24, 1724, to take his family to the St. Domingue Islands. He received approval, but officials pleaded with him to reconsider and finish construction of the church. Jacques de la Chase, a Company of the Indies official, realized that Zerhinger was the only person in the entire colony capable of constructing such a building. Members of the Superior Council of New Orleans agreed and persuaded Zerhinger to stay, giving him a quart of wine and a quart of flour as a gratuity. They also promised that he could return to France or travel to the Islands of St. Domingue with his family after one year if he still wished to leave Louisiana.[9]

On June 21, 1726, de Pauger suffered an untimely death before seeing the church he designed completed. He stated in his will that he wished to be buried within the unfinished church. His wish was presumably granted. After de Pauger's death, Zehringer completed the church.[10]

Only a few months after de Pauger's death, life took a dramatic twist for Zerhinger. On September 18, 1726, his eighteen-year-old daughter Marie Salome fell ill and died. Two months later, his wife died. Throughout this devastating time, he continued work on the church. He married Barbara Haertel, the widow of Magnus Albert (Albrecht) and Joseph Baillif (Bailly), on December 26, 1726, only a month after his second wife died. Witnesses to the marriage of Zeringher and Haertel were Jacques Jozennet, an employee of the Company of the Indies; Joseph Werret, a resident of Orleans Parish; and a person called "Saubaigne," who lived in Gentilly.[11] Barbara and Michael had four sons: Michael Jacques, Pierre Laurent, Joseph, and Jean Louis.[12]

The family surname changed slightly with time. Michael Zerhinger became known as "Michael Zeringue." The spelling of his name had been somewhat in flux in the past—from Zerhinger to Sering to Seringue and others (which was certainly very common in this era), but with time the name had somewhat cemented as

"Zeringue," although variations such as "Zerangue" and "Zyrangue" still exist today.[13]

Zerhinger stayed in Louisiana and completed the construction of the St. Louis Church, named in honor of the sainted French king, Louis IX, patron saint of Bourbon France. The church was officially dedicated on December 24, 1727, by Father Raphaël de Luxembourg, O.M. Cap., the Rector of the Parish.[14]

The nave of the church was 112 feet long, 32 feet wide, and 24 feet tall. Two bells and a clock rested in a belfry above the front entrance. There were 18 pews that were auctioned off to the highest bidders. It was customary in that era for Catholics to "pay" for their seats. This created rivalry among the worshipers, all of whom wanted excellent seats. In addition to the 18 pews, two L-shaped pews were reserved for members of the Superior Council and staff officers. There were also two armchairs near the altar, one for the governor, the other for the intendant.[15]

The church became the center of life in New Orleans: public announcements were attached to its door; births and deaths were recorded there; and residents throughout the city worshipped, celebrated, and grieved within its walls.

After the completion of the St. Louis Church, officials awarded Zerhinger a contract to construct a convent for the Ursuline nuns and an accompanying school. The Ursulines of Rouen had arrived in New Orleans on August 6, 1727, after contracting with the Company of the Indies a year before. The nuns were "to go to Louisiana . . . to take charge of the Hospital of New Orleans and to employ themselves in the education of young girls . . . His Majesty wishing to favor all that can contribute to the relief of the poor and the sick and to the education of youth . . . places them under his protection and safeguard. And for assurance of his will, His Majesty has commanded me to dispatch the present brevet which he has been pleased to sign with his own hand."[16]

The construction of the buildings lagged because of a lack of skilled laborers, but Zerhinger completed the framing of the convent by March 25, 1729, and had acquired all the wood for the completion of the structure. In a letter sent to the directors of the Company of the Indies in Paris, Company official de la Chaise and engineer Perier wrote, "Master Mikel (Seringue), who has undertaken the building of the Ursuline convent, has his timber all ready and is going to bring it here some day soon, in order to put up their buildings at once. The casement doors and the rest of the joiners' work will also be ready since it has been a year since they were begun. In spite of that, we do not think that it is possible to provide them [the Ursulines] lodgings in it before nine or 10 months, no matter how diligent we may be."[17]

Their assumption about the completion of the project was somewhat hasty. By 1731, the convent was still not complete. At this time, tiles still needed to be placed on the roof and the ground had to be filled to the proper level, but this could not be completed until the laborers were finished installing floors, steps, doors, frames, and ironwork.[18] Because of the lack of labor and other difficulties, Zerhinger was unable to complete the convent until 1734. The brick-between-posts structure was located on Arsenal Street (now named Ursuline Street in the Sisters' honor), facing the Mississippi River. The nuns, who had been residing in a rented house at the corner of Chartres and Bienville Streets, moved into their new convent on July 17, 1734. An imposing "civil, military, and religious" ceremony marked the occasion.[19] The ceremony included a grand procession, a description of which follows:

> We went out in order, having on our church veils lowered and each a
> lighted candle of white wax . . . Our Mother Superior and Assistant [were]
> near the Blessed Sacrament which was carried under a rich canopy. . . .
> [There were] twenty or twenty-five young girls dressed as angels. One of
> them represented St. Ursula. She was clothed in silver tinsel with a large
> trailing mantle of the same material, her hair dressed with ribbon of pearls
> and diamonds, a small veil flowing from her head and a superb crown. . . .
> The soldiers ranged both sides of the street marching in file in good order,
> leaving between them and us a distance of 4 feet. Their drums and fifes
> joining with the songs made an agreeable harmony.[20]

Following the soldiers, day students, orphans, members of the congregation, and clergy marched behind the procession. As the procession ended, the Sisters were most relieved finally to enter their new home.[21]

After completion of the convent, the Company of the Indies wished for Michael Zerhinger to construct the Presbytere of the Germans. The building was indeed constructed, but there is no conclusive evidence that Zerhinger built it.

Zerhinger continued to live in Louisiana and presumably continued practicing his trade. Records show that in 1731, Zeringher resided with his family—his wife and three children—below "Chapitoulas," somewhere in the Sixth District of New Orleans (part of present-day Jefferson Parish). At this time, his household possessions consisted of "one engage [indentured servant], twelve Negroes, four Negresses, and twenty-seven cows." His residence was described as being thirty by fifty feet, situated on land that was twenty-two arpents wide by the usual forty arpents deep.[22]

In less than ten years, Zeringher had truly seen New Orleans grow from a humble village of huts and shacks with only a handful of settlers along the muddy banks of the Mississippi River to a true city, with a magnificent church and streets bustling with nearly eight thousand residents. What pride he must have felt knowing that he played an integral part in making the city what it was.

Henry, the Royal Notary, visited the home of Jacques Ozenne on the morning of September 4, 1738. There he found Zerhinger very ill and in need of recording his last will and testament. When Henry completed the will, Zerhinger was too sick to sign it. He died later that evening. It is not clear why he was at the home of Ozenne at the time of his death.[23]

After her husband's death, Barbara married Louis Harang in May 1740. The marriage contract stipulated that provisions were to be made for her minor children, Michel, Pierre Laurent, Joseph, and Jean Louis Zeringue, as well as for Laurent Bailly, her son from an earlier marriage to Joseph Bailly. The contract was signed by Henry the Royal Notary. This marriage began a generations-long association between the Harang and Zeringue families.

Almost a quarter century after his father's death, Zerhinger's son Jean Louis married Marie Francois Hubert LaCroix. The 1762 ceremony took place in the St. Louis Church, which Jean Louis's father had built. That same year France agreed to cede the colony of Louisiana, and soon after New Orleans was left to Spanish control.

The 1763 census of the colony reveals that Jean Louis lived near his father's old residence on 15 arpents in the Captaincy of Chapitoulas, District of Bellair. At that time his household consisted of himself, his wife, and their daughter. The family owned twenty head of cattle, six horses and mules, fifty sheep, and two pistols.

During the course of their marriage, Jean Louis and Marie had eleven children: Eulalie, Joseph (Joachim), Honore, Michael, Mariane, Hubert, Jean Louis Jr., Ursin, Marguerite Manette, Constance, and Marie Clarice.[24]

The grand church, which Zerhinger constructed, continued to be the center of life in growing New Orleans until it was abandoned in 1763, because of a great need for repairs. During this time, priests held services in one of the King's warehouses on Dumaine Street. A partition in the warehouse was torn out, creating a large chamber where worshipers temporarily assembled until the repairs were finished on the church.[25]

On Good Friday, March 21, 1788, a large fire, which consumed a great deal of the settlement, destroyed the church. The fire started at the home of Don Jose Vicente Nunez, military treasurer of the province. Nunez, a devout Catholic, lit candles in front of a shrine in order to celebrate the feast day and a strong gust of wind blew the window curtains against the candles' flames. The entry in the Cabildo (local government) records states, "The fire started with such fury, due to the strong south wind, it was impossible to control until four hours later, during which time four-fifths of the populated section of the city was reduced to ashes, including the parish church and house, the Casa Capitular, and city jail." The fire consumed 865 houses, leaving only the buildings on the levee in front of the Mississippi River. Residents immediately began to rebuild their beloved New Orleans.[26]

A new St. Louis Church (which later become a Basilica) was built on the location of the first church by Gilberto Gullemard and his associates. Philanthropist Don Andres Almonaster Roxas financed the construction of the new church and was later buried beneath its floors. It was completed about five years after the fire.

BIBLIOGRAPHY

Allan, William. *Life and Work of John McDonogh.* Metairie, La.: Jefferson Parish Historical Commission, 1983. Monograph VI.

Andressen, Kay. Interview by the author. Kenner, La. 31 July 1999.

Andrews, Eliza Frances. *The War-Time Journal of a Georgia Girl, 1864–1865.* New York: D. Appleton and Company, 1908.

"Another deadline for Seven Oaks." *New Orleans States-Item.* 10 May 1977.

Arthur, Stanley Clisby. *Old New Orleans.* Gretna, La.: Pelican Publishing Company, 1990.

Ash, Stephen V. "Poor Whites in the Occupied South, 1861–1865." *Journal of Southern History* 57, no. 1 (Feb. 1991): 39–62.

Aykroyd, W. R. *The Story of Sugar.* Chicago: Quadrangle Books, 1967.

Ball, Edward. *Slaves in the Family.* New York: Farrar, Straus, and Giroux, 1998.

Bardaglio, Peter W. *Reconstructing the Household, Families, Sex, and the Law in the Nineteenth Century South.* Chapel Hill: University of North Carolina Press, 1995.

Barry, Fred. "7 Oaks Grant Request Okayed by Jeff Council." *New Orleans Times-Picayune.* 9 Apr. 1976.

———. "Bid to Save Mansion Accelerates." *New Orleans Times-Picayune.* 20 Mar. 1976.

———. "Demolition of Ruins Extended 6 Months." *New Orleans Times-Picayune.* 9 Nov. 1976.

———. "Fate of Seven Oaks." *New Orleans Times-Picayune.* 14 Mar. 1976.

———. "Once Splendid Orleans Mansion Now Crumbling Towards Death." *New Orleans Times-Picayune.* 26 July 1970.

———. "Seven Oaks." *New Orleans Times-Picayune.* 29 Feb. 1976.

———. "Seven Oaks Finale." *New Orleans Times-Picayune.* 24 Oct. 1976.

———. "State Funds Available to Restore Seven Oaks." *New Orleans Times-Picayune.* 6 Apr. 1976.

Baudier, Roger. *The Catholic Church in Louisiana.* New Orleans, 1939. Reprinted by the Louisiana Library Association, Public Library Section, 1972.

Beauford, Gertrude M. "A Tribute to Derbigny." *Jefferson History Notebook* vol. 2, no. 1. (Mar, 1980).

Becnel, Thomas A. *The Barrow Family and the Barataria and Lafourche Canal: The Transportation Revolution in Louisiana, 1829–1925.* Baton Rouge: Louisiana State University Press, 1989.

Begnaud, Allen. "The Louisiana Sugar Cane Industry." In *Green Fields: Two Hundred Years of Louisiana Sugar.* Lafayette: The Center for Louisiana Studies, University of Southwestern Louisiana, 1980.

Bergeron, Arthur W., Jr. *Guide to Louisiana Confederate Military Units, 1861–1865.* Baton Rouge: Louisiana State University Press, 1989.

Bezou, Henry C. "Carrollton: East Jefferson's Last Lost Property." *Jefferson History Notebook* vol. 3, no. 1 (Sept. 1984).

———, ed. *Jefferson Parish Historical Markers.* Harahan, La.: Jefferson Parish Historical Commission, 1987. Monograph X.

———, ed. *Random Readings—The Jefferson Parish Yearly Review.* Metairie, La.: Jefferson Parish Historical Commission, 1985. Monograph VIII.

Bibb, Henry. *Narrative of the Life and Adventures of Henry Bibb, An American Slave.* New York: Published by Henry Bibb, 1849.

Bolner, James, ed. *Louisiana Politics: Festival in a Labyrinth.* Baton Rouge: Louisiana State University Press, 1982.

Borne, Frank J., Jr. *Jefferson Parish Politicians of the Past and Present: 1825–2001.* Published by Frank J. Borne Jr., 2001.

Bouchereau, A. *Statement of the Sugar and Rice Crops Made in Louisiana in 1881–82.* New Orleans: L. Graham and Sons, Printers, 1882.

Bouchereau, L. *Statement of the Sugar and Rice Crops Made in Louisiana in 1872–73.* New Orleans: Pelican Book and Job Printing Office, 1873.

Brehm, Loretta Persohn. Interview with the author. 2001.

Brooks, Philip C. "Spain's Farewell to Louisiana, 1803–1821." *Mississippi Valley Historical Review* 27, no. 1 (June 1940): 29–42.

Brown, William W. *Narrative of William W. Brown, An American Slave.* London: Charles Gilpin, Bishopgate-St. Without, 1849.

Bruce, Edwin Ney. "Westwego, Louisiana: A Community Study". Master's Thesis, Tulane University, Thesis Collection, vol. 2, 1947.

Bruns, J. Edgar. *Archbishop Antoine Blanc Memorial.* New Orleans: The Roman Catholic Church of the Archdiocese of New Orleans, 1981.

Butler, W. E. *Down Among the Sugarcane.* Baton Rouge: Moran Publishing Corporation, 1990.

Cable, Mary. *Lost New Orleans.* Boston: Houghton Mifflin Company, 1980.

Carleton, Mark T., Perry H. Howard, and Joseph B. Parker, eds. *Readings in Louisiana Politics.* Baton Rouge: Claitor's Publishing Division, 1975.

Champomier, P. A. *Statement of the Sugar Crop Made in Louisiana in 1849–50.* New Orleans: Cook, Young and Company, 1850.

———. *Statement of the Sugar Crop Made in Louisiana in 1853–54.* New Orleans: Cook, Young and Company, 1854.

Chestnut, Mary. *A Diary from Dixie*. New York: Gramercy Books, 1997.

Ciravolo, G. Leighton. *The Legacy of John McDonogh*. Lafayette: The Center for Louisiana Studies, University of Louisiana at Lafayette, 2002.

Clinton, Catherine. *The Plantation Mistress*. New York: Pantheon Books, 1982.

Clinton, Catherine, and Michele Gillespie, eds. *The Devil's Lane: Sex and Race in the Early South*. New York: Oxford University Press, 1997.

"Columbia Gardens." *New Orleans Daily Picayune*. 24 May 1893.

Conrad, Glenn R., ed. *Readings in Louisiana History*. New Orleans: The Louisiana Historical Association in cooperation with The Center for Louisiana Studies, University of Southwestern Louisiana, 1978.

Conrad, Glenn R., and Ray F. Lucas. *White Gold: A Brief History of The Louisiana Sugar Industry 1795–1995*. Lafayette: The Center for Louisiana Studies, University of Southwestern Louisiana, 1995.

Cooper, F. Wesley. *Louisiana: A Treasure of Plantation Homes*. Natchez, Miss.: Southern Historical Publications, Inc., 1961.

Cooper, William J., Jr. *Liberty and Slavery: Southern Politics to 1860*. New York: McGraw-Hill Publishing Company, 1983.

Corley, Dawson. "137 Years of History." *Baton Rouge State Times*. 13 Oct. 1978.

Crété, Liliane. *Daily Life in Louisiana, 1815–1830*. Translated by Patrick Gregory. Baton Rouge: Louisiana State University Press, 1981.

Curry, Mary Grace. "Gretna: A Sesquicentennial Salute." Metairie, La.: Jefferson Parish Historical Commission, 1986. Monograph IX.

———. "Jefferson Parish Courthouses." *Jefferson History Notebook* vol. 6, no. 2 (July 2002).

Curry, Mary Grace, and Charmaine Currault Rini, eds. "Jefferson Parish Events 1825–2000." Harahan, La.: Jefferson Parish Historical Commission, 2000.

De Conde, Alexander. *This Affair of Louisiana*. Baton Rouge: Louisiana State University Press, 1976.

Deiler, John Hanno. *The Settlement of the German Coast of Louisiana and the Creoles of German Descent*. Updated by Jack Belson. Baltimore: Genealogical Publishing Company, 1969.

"Demolition Delay OK'd." *New Orleans Times-Picayune*. 6 July 1977.

Dew, Charles B. "Who Won the Succession Election in Louisiana?" *Journal of Southern History* 36, no. 1 (Feb. 1970): 18–32.

"Did You Know?" *Transt Riders' Digest*. 10 May 1976.

"Died Zerinque" (sic). Obituary. *New Orleans Daily Picayune*. 7 Jan. 1872.

Din, Gilbert C. *Francisco Bouligny: A Bourbon Soldier in Spanish Louisiana*. Baton Rouge: Louisiana State University Press, 1993.

Donaldson, Gary A. "A Window on Slave Culture: Dances at Congo Square in New Orleans, 1800–1862." *Journal of Negro History* 69, no. 2 (Spring 1984): 63–72.

Dufour, Pie. "Preview of Seven Oaks." *New Orleans Times-Picayune*. 5 May 1957.

Dusinberre, William. *Them Dark Days: Slavery in the American Rice Swamps.* Athens: University of Georgia Press, 2000.

Eichstedt, Jennifer L., and Stephen Small. *Representations of Slavery: Race and Ideology in Southern Plantation Museums.* Washington, D.C.: Smithsonian Institution Press, 2002.

Equiano, Olaudah. *The Interesting Narrative of the Life of Olaudah Equiano, or Gustavus Vassa, the African. Written by Himself.* 2 vols. London: Published by Olaudah Equiano, 1789.

Estaville, Lawrence E., Jr. *Confederate Neckties: Louisiana Railroads in the Civil War.* Ruston, La.: McGinty Publications, 1989.

Evans, Oliver. *New Orleans.* New York: MacMillian Company, 1959.

Evans, Sally Kittredge, Frederick Stielow, and Betsy Swanson. *Grand Isle on the Gulf: An Early History.* Metairie, La.: Jefferson Parish Historical Commission, 1981.

Everett, James. "Seven Oaks." *Clarion Herald.* 13 Mar. 1969.

Ferleger, Louis. "Farm Mechanization in the Southern Sugar Section After the Civil War." *Louisiana History* 23 (Winter 1982): 21–34.

————. "The problem of 'labor' in the post-Reconstruction Louisiana sugar industry." (African Americans in Southern Agriculture: 1877–1945). *Agricultural History* 72, no. 2 (Spring 1998).

Fischer, Roger A. "Racial Segregation in Ante Bellum New Orleans." *American Historical Review* 74, no. 3 (Feb. 1969): 926–37.

Follett, Richard J. "The Sugar Masters: Slavery, Economic Development, and Modernization on Louisiana Sugar Plantations, 1820–1860." Ph.D. dissertation, Louisiana State University, Baton Rouge, 1997.

Foreman, Agnes Rita Zeringue. *Zerangue, Zeringue, Zyrangue and Allied Families.* Baltimore: Gateway Press, Inc. 1979.

Fortier, Alcée. *A History of Louisiana.* Multi-volume set. 2nd ed. by Mark T. Carleton. Baton Rouge: Claitor's Publishing Divison, 1985.

Foshee, Andrew W. "Slave Hiring in Rural Louisiana." *Louisiana History* 26 (Winter 1985): 63–73.

Fox-Genovese, Elizabeth. *Within the Plantation Household.* Chapel Hill: University of North Carolina Press, 1988.

Frazer, Tom. "Seven Oaks Plantation torn down, carted off." *New Orleans States-Item.* 30 Aug. 1977.

Frey, Sylvia R. *Water From the Rock.* Princeton: Princeton University Press, 1991.

Frey, Sylvia R., and Betty Wood. *Come Shouting to Zion: African American Protestantism in the American South and British Caribbean to 1830.* Chapel Hill: University of North Carolina Press, 1998.

Gayarré, Charles. *History of Louisiana.* Republished. New Orleans: Pelican Publishing Company, 1965.

Giardina, Anthony. Telephone interview by the author. July 2001.

Giardina, Lloyd F. Interview by the author. 21 June 2001.

Giraud, Marcel. *A History of French Louisiana, Vol. 5, The Company of the Indies, 1723–1731*. Translated by Brian Pearce. Baton Rouge: Louisiana State University Press, 1991.

Gleason, David King. *Plantation Homes of Louisiana and the Natchez Area*. Baton Rouge: Louisiana State University Press, 1982.

Golay, Michael. *Reconstruction and Reaction*. New York: Facts on File, 1996.

"Golden Jubilee, 1920–1970." Booklet. Westwego: Our Lady of Prompt Succor Church, 1970.

Goodwin, Christopher R., Jill-Karen Yakubik, and Cyd Heymann Goodwin. *Elmwood: The Historic Archeology of a Southeastern Louisiana Plantation*. Metairie, La.: Jefferson Parish Historical Commission, 1984.

Gore, Laura Locoul. *Memories of the Old Plantation Home*. Vacherie, La.: Zoë Company, Inc., 2001.

Green Fields: Two Hundred Years of Louisiana Sugar. Lafayette: The Center for Louisiana Studies, University of Southwestern Louisiana, 1980.

Hair, William Ivy. *Bourbonism and Agrarian Protest: Louisiana Politics, 1877–1900*. Baton Rouge: Louisiana State University Press, 1969.

Hall, Gwendolyn Midlo. *Africans in Colonial Louisiana*. Baton Rouge: Louisiana State University Press, 1992.

———. *Afro-Louisiana History and Genealogy, 1718–1820*. Database. www.ibiblio.org/laslave/

Harris, Mildred Stehle. Interview by the author. Nine Mile Point, La., Sept. 2000.

———. Lecture Presentation. Jefferson Historical Society of Louisiana Quarterly Meeting. 8 Dec. 1999.

Hawks, Joanne V., and Shelia L. Skemp, eds. *Sex, Race, and the Role of Women in the South*. Jackson: University Press of Mississippi, 1983.

"Heritage Artist Paints Seven Oaks Plantation in New Orleans." *Daily Iberian*. 21 Sept. 1971.

Holmes, Jack D. L. "Indigo in Colonial Louisiana and the Floridas." *Louisiana History* 8 (Fall 1967): 329–49.

———. "The Value of the Arpent in Spanish Louisiana and West Florida." *Louisiana History* 24 (Summer 1983): 314–20.

Hosch, Robert Jr. "Plantation restoration is key." Letter to the editor. *New Orleans Times-Picayune*. 2 Aug. 2003. B-6.

Howard, Robert West, ed. *This Is the South*. Chicago: Rand McNally & Company, 1959.

Huber, Leonard V., and Samuel Wilson Jr. *The Basilica on Jackson Square*. New Orleans: Saint Louis Cathedral, 1965.

Ingersoll, Thomas N. "Free Blacks in a Slave Society: New Orleans, 1718–1812." *William and Mary Quarterly*, 3rd series. 48, no. 2 (Apr. 1991): 173–200.

Jachcke, Davis. Interview by the author. New Orleans, July 2001.

Jackson, Lily. "Old South, New Address." *New Orleans Times-Picayune*. 17 Dec. 1993.

"Jeff Council Hit by Alario." *New Orleans Times-Picayune*. 13 Apr. 1976.

"Jeff Council Turns Back on Seven Oaks Home." *New Orleans Times-Picayune*. 10 Sept. 1976.

"Jeff Plans to Preserve Seven Oaks." *New Orleans Times-Picayune*. 26 Mar. 1976.

"Jesse James Deleted in Mansion Resolution." *New Orleans Times-Picayune*. 21 Aug. 1976.

Jones, Katharine M. *The Plantation South*. Indianapolis: Bobbs-Merrill Company, Inc., 1957.

Jung, Moon-Ho. "'Coolies' and Cane: Race, Labor, and Sugar Production in Louisiana, 1852–1877." Ph.D. dissertation, Cornell University, 2000.

Kahn, Louis. "On Architecture for Academia." *Fortune*. May 1963.

Kaiser, Keith. "Effort Will Be Made to Restore Ancient Mansion." *West Bank Guide*. 21 June 1967.

Kane, Harnett T. *Plantation Parade: The Grand Manner in Louisiana*. New York: Bonanza Books, 1945.

Kolchin, Peter. *American Slavery, 1619–1877*. New York: Hill and Wang, 1993.

Kukla, Jon. *A Wilderness So Immense*. New York: Alfred A. Knopf, 2003.

Lane, Mills. *Architecture of the Old South Louisiana*. New York: Abbeville Press Publishers, 1990.

Le Gardeur, René J., Jr. "The Origins of the Sugar Industry in Louisiana." In *Green Fields: Two Hundred Years of Louisiana Sugar*. Lafayette: The Center for Louisiana Studies, University of Southwestern Louisiana, 1980.

Lettres Anuelles, 1921–23, 2:348–49, Society of the Sacred Heart National Archives.

Lettres Anuelles, 1924–26, 2:345–51, Society of the Sacred Heart National Archives.

Lettres Anuelles, 1927–29, 2:340–44, Society of the Sacred Heart National Archives.

Louisiana Plantation Homes. Baton Rouge Department of Commerce and Industry, 1961.

Louisiana Purchase. exhibition guide. New Orleans: Louisiana State Museum and The Louisiana Landmarks Society, 1953.

"Madeline Lisa (sic) Roman Zeringue." Obituary. *New Orleans Daily Picayune*. 17 Apr. 1892.

Madere, Beverly Anne. "Three Centuries on Nine Mile Point: Patterns of Ownership and Land Utilization." Thesis, University of New Orleans, 1998.

Malone, Ann Patton. *Sweet Chariot: Slave Family and Household Structure in Nineteenth-Century Louisiana*. Chapel Hill: University of North Carolina Press, 1992.

Margavio, A. V., and Jerome J. Salomone. *Bread and Respect, The Italians of Louisiana.* Gretna, La.: Pelican Publishing, 2002.

Martin, Fontaine. *A History of the Bouligny Family and Allied Families.* The Center for Louisiana Studies, University of Southwestern Louisiana, 1990.

Matrana, Marc R. "Old mansion gone forever." Letter to the editor. *New Orleans Times-Picayune.* 9 Aug. 2003. B-6.

————. "On Cane and Coolies: Chinese Laborers on Post-Antebellum Louisiana Sugar Plantations As Exemplified on the Millaudon Plantation of Jefferson Parish". *Jefferson History Notebook* 7, no. 1 (Feb. 2003).

————. "Seven Oaks Plantation: A Lasting Legacy, The 25th Anniversary of the Demolition." *Jefferson History Notebook* 6, no. 1 (Feb. 2002).

McDonald, Roderick A. *The Economy and Material Culture of Slaves: Goods and Chattels on the Sugar Plantations of Jamaica and Louisiana.* Baton Rouge: Louisiana State University Press, 1993.

McGoldrick, Stacy K. "The Policing of Slavery in New Orleans, 1852–1860." *Journal of Historical Sociology* 14, no. 4 (Dec. 2001): 397–417.

McMillan, John. "Capote vs. Seven Oaks." *Dixie Roto Magizine, New Orleans Times-Picayune.* 17 June 1973. p. 10.

Menn, Joseph Karl. *The Large Slaveholders of Louisiana—1860.* New Orleans: Pelican Publishing Company, 1964.

Miller, Herschel. "Goodbye Seven Oaks." *New Orleans.* May 1969. 28–31.

Millet, Donald J. "The Saga of Water Transportation into Southwest Louisiana to 1900." *Louisiana History* 15 (Fall 1974): 339–56.

Mintz, Sidney W. "Sweetness and Power: The Place of Sugar in Modern History." New York: Viking Penguin, Inc., 1985.

Moody, V. A. "Slavery on Louisiana Sugar Plantations." *Louisiana Historical Quarterly* 7 (Apr. 1924): 191–303.

Mullin, Gerald W. *Flight and Rebellion: Slave Resistance in Eighteenth-Century Virginia.* London: Oxford University Press, 1975.

"News of Some of the Plantation Houses in Southern Louisiana." *Préservation.* Louisiana Landmarks Society. Mar. 1958.

Northup, Solomon. *Twelve Years a Slave.* Ed. by Sue Eakin and Joseph Logsdon. Baton Rouge: Louisiana State University Press, 1968.

Overdyke, W. Darrell. *Louisiana Plantation Homes, Colonial and Ante Bellum.* New York: Architectural Book Publishing Company, Inc., 1965.

Parker, Sheryl H. "Seven Oaks Plantation." Academic Paper. Special Collections of Tulane University; New Orleans, n.d.

Peña, Christopher G., *Touched by War: Battles Fought in the Lafourche District.* Thibodaux, La.: C.G.P. Press, 1998.

Phillips, Ulrich B. *Life and Labor in the Old South.* Boston: Little, Brown and Company, 1963.

Pitts, Stella. "Seven Oaks in Westwego is on Path to Disintegration." *New Orleans Times-Picayune.* 14 Apr. 1974.

"Plea for Seven Oaks Goes to Panel." *New Orleans Times-Picayune.* 27 July 1976.

Poesch, Jessie, and Barbara Bacot. *Louisiana Buildings, 1720–1940.* Baton Rouge: Louisiana State University Press, 1997.

———. "A Forward Step for Jeff History?" *New Orleans States-Item.* 19 Jan. 1977.

Pope, John. "Don Lee Keith, 62, writer, instructor." Obituarary. *New Orleans Times-Picayune.* 30 July 2003.

———. "History is Bulldozed at Seven Oaks." *New Orleans States-Item.* 5 Sept. 1977.

———. "Hope Among the Ruins?" *New Orleans States-Item.* 13 Mar. 1976.

———. "Land Acquisition May Save Mansion." *New Orleans States-Item.* 20 Mar. 1976.

———. "Politics and the Plantation." *New Orleans States-Item.* 17 Apr. 1976.

———. "River Mansion Traces Doom." *New Orleans States-Item.* 27 Feb. 1976.

———. "Seven Oaks Safe for Now." *New Orleans States-Item.* 27 Nov. 1976.

———. "Seven Oaks wins stay of execution." *New Orleans States-Item.* 9 Nov. 1976.

———. "Stay of execution may save 7 Oaks." *New Orleans States-Item.* 6 Nov. 1976.

———. "When it was home . . ." *New Orleans States-Item.* 6 June 1977. sec. B.

———. "Wilting Seven Oaks May be Saved by State." *New Orleans States-Item.*

Prichard, Walter. "The Effects of the Civil War on the Louisiana Sugar Industry." *Journal of Southern History* 5, no. 3 (Aug. 1939): 315–32.

———. "A Forgotten Louisiana Engineer: G. W. R. Bayley and His 'History of the Railroads of Louisiana.'" *Louisiana Historical Quarterly* 30 (Oct. 1947): 1065–1325.

———. "Routine on a Louisiana Sugar Plantation under the Slavery Regime." *Mississippi Valley Historical Review* 14, no. 2 (Sept. 1927): 168–78.

Prichett, Jonathan B., and Herman Freudenberger. "A Peculiar Sample: The Selection of Slaves for the New Orleans Market." *Journal of Economic History* 52, no. 1 (Mar. 1992): 109–27.

Raphael, Morris. *The Battle in Bayou Country.* New Iberia, La.: Morris Raphael Books, 1975.

Reeves, William D. *De La Barre: Life of a French Creole Family in Louisiana.* New Orleans: Jefferson Parish Historical Commission, 1980. Monograph IV.

Reeves, William D., with Daniel Alario Sr. *Westwego, From Cheniere to Canal.* Westwego, La.: Published Privately by Mr. and Mrs. Daniel Alario Sr., 1996.

Rehder, John B. *Delta Sugar: Louisiana's Vanishing Plantation Landscape.* Baltimore: Johns Hopkins University Press, 1999.

Reidy, Joseph P. "Mules and Machines and Men: Field Labor on Louisiana Sugar Plantations, 1887–1915." (African Americans in Southern Agriculture: 1877–1945). *Agricultural History* 72, no. 2 (Spring 1998).

Ricciuti, Italo William. *New Orleans and Its Environs: The Domestic Architecture, 1727–1870.* New York: Bonanza Books, 1938.

Robertson, James I., Jr. *The History of the Civil War*. Conshohocken, Penn.: Eastern Acorn Press, 1979.

Robichaux, Albert J., Jr. *German Coast Families: European Origins and Settlement in Colonial Louisiana*. Rayne, La.: Hebert Publications, 1997.

Rodrigue, John C. *Reconstruction in the Cane Fields: From Slavery to Free Labor in Louisiana's Sugar Parishes, 1862–1880*. Baton Rouge: Louisiana State University Press, 2001.

Roland, Charles P. *Louisiana Sugar Plantations During the American Civil War*. Leiden: E. J. Brill, 1957.

Rudd, Robert Mark. "Apocryphal Grandeur: Belle Grove Plantation in Iberville Parish, Louisiana." Master's thesis, University of Delaware, 2002.

"Save 7 Oaks Call Heeded." *New Orleans Times-Picayune*. 8 Apr. 1976.

Schafer, Judith Kelleher. "New Orleans Slavery in 1850 as Seen in Advertisements." *Journal of Southern History* 47, no. 1 (Feb. 1981): 33–56.

————. *Slavery, the Civil Law, and the Supreme Court of Louisiana*. Baton Rouge: Louisiana State University Press, 1994.

Schilke, Harold. *One Hundred Years of Public Welfare Administration by the Police Jury of Jefferson Parish, Louisiana*. Master's thesis, 1937, Tulane University Archives, New Orleans, Louisiana.

Seebold, Herman de Bachelle, M.D. *Old Louisiana Plantation Homes and Family Trees*, vol. 1. New Orleans: Pelican Press, 1941.

"Seven Oaks." *Préservation*. Louisiana Landmarks Society. Mar. 1957.

"Seven Oaks." *Préservation*. Louisiana Landmarks Society. July 1958.

"Seven Oaks." *New Orleans Times-Picayune*. 29 Feb. 1976.

"Seven Oaks 1840–1977." *Préservation*. Louisiana Landmarks Society. Nov. 1977.

"Seven Oaks Is Denied Federal Aid." *New Orleans Times-Picayune*. 2 Sept. 1976.

"Seven Oaks Last Chance." *Dixie*. 14 May 1972.

"Seven Oaks Mansion in Westwego Crumbling." *New Orleans Times-Picayune*. 22 Feb. 1967.

"Seven Oaks Torn Down." *New Orleans Times-Picayune*. 31 Aug. 1977.

"Seven Oaks Plantation, Westwego: The Roof's On—What Next?" *Préservation*. Louisiana Landmarks Society. Aug. 1957.

Shugg, Roger Wallace. "Survival of the Plantation System in Louisiana." *Journal of Southern History* 3, no. 3 (Aug. 1937): 311–25.

Sifakis, Stewart. *Compendium of the Confederate Armies—Louisiana*. New York: Facts on File, 1995.

Sitterson, J. Carlye. *Sugar Country: The Sugar Cane Industry in the South, 1753–1950*. Lexington: University of Kentucky Press, 1953.

Smedes, Susan Dabney. *Memorials of a Southern Planter*. Baltimore: Cushings & Bailey, 1887.

Spratling, William P., and Natalie Vivian Scott. *Old Plantation Houses in Louisiana*. New York: William Helburn Inc., 1927.

Starobin, Robert S., ed. *Blacks in Bondage: Letters of American Slaves*. New York: Barnes and Nobles Books, 1998. Reprint.

"State Landmarks Group Sets N.O. Meet Tomorrow." *Baton Rouge State Times*. 27 May 1969.

Styron, William. *The Confessions of Nat Turner*. New York: Vintage International, 1993.

Sternberg, Mary Ann. *Along the River Road: Past and Present on Louisiana's Historic Byway*. Baton Rouge: Louisiana State University Press, 1996.

Stroyer, Jacob. *My Life in the South*. Salem, Mass., 1898.

Swanson, Betsy. *Historic Jefferson Parish, From Shore to Shore*. Gretna, La.: Pelican Publishing, 1975.

———. "Seven Oaks: Lost Forever?" *New Orleans States-Item*. 30 Oct. 1976.

———. Telephone interviews by the author. 17 Aug. 2001 and 19 Jan. 2004.

———. *Terre Haute De Barataria*. Harahan, La.: Jefferson Parish Historical Commission, 1991. Monograph XI.

———. "What Will Happen to Seven Oaks?" *Friends of the Cabildo Newsletter*. Dec. 1976.

Swanson, Betsy, and Bethlyn MsCloskey. "The Saga of Seven Oaks". *Préservation*. Louisiana Landmarks Society. Oct. 1976. 1+.

———. "Seven Oaks: Hope, Despair, and Hope Again." Abbreviated version. *Préservation*. Louisiana Landmarks Society. July 1976. 4+.

Taylor, Joe Gray. "Slavery in Louisiana During the Civil War." *Louisiana History* 8 (Winter 1967): 27–34.

Thoede, Henry J. *History of Jefferson Parish and Its People*. Gretna, La.: Distinctive Printing, 1976.

Toledano, Roulhac. "It's Not Too Late To Save Seven Oaks Plantation." *Figaro*. 17 Mar. 1976. 8.

———. "Louisiana's Golden Age: Valcour Aime in St. James Parish." *Louisiana History* 10 (Summer 1969): 211–24.

Tolzman, Don Heinrich. *Louisiana's German Heritage*. Bowie, Md.: Hertiage Books, Inc., 1994.

Treadway, Joan. "Plantation Must Go—Unless." *New Orleans Times-Picayune*. 10 May 1977.

Tregle, Joseph G., Jr., trans. *The History of Louisiana*, by M. Le Page du Pratz. Baton Rouge: Louisiana State Univeristy Press. 1975.

"Trespassing Permitted . . . Today Only." *Dixie Roto, New Orleans Times-Picayune*. 11 May 1958. p. 28+.

"Update of Seven Oaks Plantation House." *Préservation*. Louisiana Landmarks Society. Feb. 1977.

Usner Daniel H. Jr. *Indians, Settlers, and Slaves in a Frontier Exchange Economy: The Lower Mississippi Before 1783*. Chapel Hill: University of North Carolina Press, 1992.

Vandal, Gilles. "Black Violence in Post-Civil War Louisiana." *Journal of Inter-disciplinary History* 25, no. 1 (Summer 1994): 45–64.

Vlach, John Michael. *Back of the Big House: The Architecture of Plantation Slavery.* Chapel Hill: University of North Carolina Press, 1993.

———. "The Plantation Tradition in an Urban Setting: The Case of the Aiken-Rhett House in Charleston, South Carolina." *Southern Cultures* 5.4 (Winter 1999).

Wall, Bennett H., Light Townsend Cummins, and Judith Kelleher Schafer, eds. *Louisiana, A History.* 2nd ed. Arlington Heights, Ill.: Forum Press, 1990.

Wardlaw, Jack. "Terminal illness hits Seven Oaks." *New Orleans States-Item.* 29 July 1976.

"Wego Board Agrees to Back Restoration." *New Orleans Times-Picayune.* 13 Apr. 1976.

Westwego, Formerly Known as The Company Canal. Vertical Files of the Westwego Branch of the Jefferson Parish Public Library.

Whitbread, Leslie George. *Placenames of Jefferson Parish, Louisiana: An Introductory Account.* Metairie, La.: Jefferson Parish Historical Commission, 1977. Monograph 1.

White, Deborah Gray. *Ar'n't I a Woman? Female Slaves in the Plantation South.* Rev. ed. New York: W. W. Norton and Company, 1999.

Wiggins, D. "Good Times On the Old Plantation: Popular Recreations Of The Black Slave In Antebellum South, 1810–1860." *Journal of Sport History* 4, no. 3 (Fall 1977).

Williams, James. *James Williams, an American Slave, Who Was for Several Years a Driver on a Cotton Plantation in Alabama.* New York: The American Anti-Slavery Society, 1838.

Willie, Leroy E. *German Ancestors and Patriots of Louisiana.* Baton Rouge: General Philemon Thomas Chapter, Sons of the American Revolution, 1996.

Wilson, Samuel Jr. "Architecture of Early Sugar Plantations." In *Green Fields: Two Hundred Years of Louisiana Sugar.* Lafayette: The Center for Louisiana Studies, University of Southwestern Louisiana, 1980.

———. *Bienville's New Orleans: A French Colonial Capital, 1718–1768.* New Orleans: The Friends of the Cabildo, n.d.

———. "Famous La. Plantation Mansion Crumbling to Ruins Across River." *New Orleans States-Item.* 14 Nov. 1953.

———. *A Guide to Early Architecture of New Orleans.* New Orleans: American Institute of Architects.

———. "Seven Oaks Plantation." Historic American Buildings Survey. 1953.

Winters, John D. *The Civil War in Louisiana.* Reprint. Baton Rouge: Louisiana State University Press, 1991.

Wood, Betty. *The Origins of American Slavery.* New York: Hill and Wang, 1997.

Woodward, C. Vann. *The Burden of Southern History*. New York: Vintage Books, 1960.

Wyatt-Brown, Bertram. *Honor and Violence in the Old South*. Oxford: Oxford University Press, 1986.

Yetman, Norman R. *Voices From Slavery*. Mineola, N.Y.: Dover Publications, 2000.

"Youth and Age." *Dixie*. 5 Apr. 1964.

Zollman, Peter M. "Plantation Object of Preservation Drive." *Alexandria Daily Town Talk*. 11 Apr. 1976.

NOTES

Introduction

1. Now "Bridge City Avenue."
2. Samuel Wilson Jr. "Seven Oaks Plantation," Historic American Buildings Survey, 1953, HABS, Library of Congress; Samuel Wilson Jr., "Famous La. Plantation Mansion Crumbling Across River," *New Orleans States-Item*, 14 Nov. 1953.
3. Fred Barry, "Once Splendid Orleans Mansion Now Crumbling Toward Death," *New Orleans Times-Picayune*, 26 May 1970.; Dawson Corley, "137 Years of History," *Baton Rouge State Times*, 13 Oct. 1978.
4. Ibid.
5. William D. Reeves with Daniel P. Alario Sr., *Westwego, From Cheniere to Canal* (Westwego, La.: Published privately by Mr. and Mrs. Daniel Alario Sr., Jefferson Parish Historical Commission Monograph XIV, 1996), 22.

Chapter 1

1. Bennett H. Wall et al., *Louisiana, A History* (Arlington Heights, Ill.: Forum Press, 1990), 3.
2. Gwendolyn Midlo Hall, *Africans in Colonial Louisiana* (Baton Rouge: Louisiana State University Press, 1992), 2.
3. A livre, a form of currency formerly used in France, was worth a pound of silver.
4. Chaouachas later became known as Concession Plantation.
5. Corley; Samuel Wilson Jr., "Seven Oaks Plantation," HABS; Stella Pitts, "Seven Oaks in Westwego is on Path to Disintegration," *New Orleans Times-Picayune*, 14 Apr. 1974.
6. Samuel Wilson Jr., "Seven Oaks Plantation," HABS.
7. Samuel Wilson Jr. (1911–1993), known as the "dean of architectural preservation in New Orleans" was a famed Louisiana architect, historian, and scholar. A graduate of Tulane University, he was actively involved in preservation of numerous structures, and his list of publications on the subject of Louisiana's architectural heritage and history is impressive.

His zeal for Seven Oaks was obvious, and his primary research into the plantation's early history was meticulous and has been valuable to this volume and other studies.

8. Leslie George Whitbread, *Placenames of Jefferson Parish, Louisiana: An Introductory Account* (Metairie, La.: Jefferson Parish Historical Commission, 1977), 17.

9. J. Edgar Bruns, Archbishop *Antoine Blanc Memorial* (New Orleans: The Roman Catholic Church of the Archdiocese of New Orleans, 1981), 7–8.

10. Betsy Swanson, *Historic Jefferson Parish, From Shore to Shore* (Gretna, La.: Pelican Publishing, 1975), 85.

11. Pierre de Rigaud, Marquis de Vaudreuil de Cabagnial (1698–1778) served as French Governor of Louisiana from 1743 to 1752.

12. Wilson, "Seven Oaks Plantation," HABS.

13. Wall et al., 85.

14. Hall, *Africans in Colonial Louisiana*, 29; David Rider, *Slavery in Early Louisiana*; http://www.dickshovel.com/slavery.html

15. Wilson, "Seven Oaks Plantation," HABS.

16. Ibid., 10.

17. Hall, *Africans in Colonial Louisiana*, 15.

18. Wall, 77–78.

19. Wilson, "Seven Oaks Plantation." HABS; Swanson, *Historic Jefferson Parish*, 83–86.

20. Wilson, "Seven Oaks Plantation," HABS; Betsy Swanson, interview by the author, 19 Jan. 2004.

21. Reeves with Alario, 22.

22. Swanson, *Historic Jefferson Parish*; Wilson, "Seven Oaks Plantation," HABS; Thomas A. Becnel, *The Barrow Family and the Barataria and Lafourche Canal: The Transportation Revolution in Louisiana, 1829–1925* (Baton Rouge: Louisiana State University Press, 1989), 28–30; Besty Swanson, interview by the author, 19 Jan. 2004.

23. Ibid.

24. Ibid.

25. Wilson, "Seven Oaks Plantation," HABS; Louisiana Historical Quarterly. Index to Spanish Judicial Records.

26. Wilson, "Seven Oaks Plantation," HABS.; Reeves with Alario, 22–23.

27. Wilson, "Seven Oaks Plantation," HABS.; Swanson, *Historic Jefferson Parish*, 85.

28. Besty Swanson, interview by the author, 19 Jan. 2004.

29. Gwendolyn Midlo Hall, *Afro-Louisiana History and Genealogy 1718–1820*. Database: www.ibiblio.org/laslave/individ.php?sid=21970

30. Wilson, "Seven Oaks Plantation," HABS.

31. Also known as "Big Temple."

32. Reeves with Alario, 5–6. Betsy Swanson, interview by the author, 19 Jan. 2004.

Chapter 2

1. John McDonogh (1779–1850) was born in Baltimore, Maryland, and arrived in New Orleans as an apprentice merchant in 1800. He served as a director of the Louisiana Bank and became one of the most successful businessmen in Louisiana. He died in New Orleans and left his vast fortune to New Orleans and Baltimore for educational enterprises. By 1899, there were twenty-eight schools bearing John McDonogh's name in the New Orleans area. See William Allan, *Life and Work of John McDonogh* (Metairie, La.: Jefferson Parish Historical Commission, 1983). Monograph VI, and G. Leighton Ciravolo, *The Legacy of John McDonogh* (Lafayette: Center for Louisiana Studies, University of Louisiana at Lafayette, 2002).
2. Anna Constance Constant married Jean Louis Zeringue on February 6, 1797. She was the daughter of Joseph Constant and Margaret Bujol.
3. Reeves with Alario, 23; Agnes Rita Zeringue Foreman, *Zerangue, Zeringue, Zyrangue and Allied Families* (Baltimore: Gateway Press, Inc. 1979).
4. Ibid.
5. Wilson, "Famous La. Plantation Mansion Crumbling to Ruins Across River."
6. Liliane Crété, *Daily Life in Louisiana, 1815–1830*, translated in 1981 by Patrick Gregory from *La vie quotidienne en Louisiane, 1815–1830* (Baton Rouge: Louisiana State University Press, 1981), 114.
7. Ibid.
8. Jefferson Parish Judicial Records.
9. Catherine Clinton, *The Plantation Mistress* (New York: Pantheon Books, 1982), 76–77.
10. Richard J. Follett, "The Sugar Masters: Slavery, Economic Development, and Modernization on Louisiana Sugar Plantations, 1820–1860," Ph.D. dissertation, Louisiana State University, Baton Rouge, 1997.
11. Charles Zenon Derbigny, son of Louisiana governor Pierre Derbigny, built the Derbigny Plantation House, which still stands along River Road in Westwego. See Gertrude M. Beauford, "A Tribute to Derbigny," *Jefferson History Notebook*, vol. 2, no. 1, Mar. 1980.
12. The original seat of government of Jefferson Parish was at Lafayette in present-day New Orleans. The parish seat was moved to Carrollton in 1852, also in present-day New Orleans. In 1874, the parish seat was moved to Harvey; then in May 1884, it was moved to Gretna, where it remains today. Also, for an in-depth study on Jefferson Parish's governmental seats and courthouses, see "Jefferson Parish Courthouses" by Dr. Mary Grace Curry, *Jefferson History Notebook*, vol. 6, no. 2, July 2002.
13. *Westwego*, from the Vertical Files of the Westwego Branch of the Jefferson Parish Public Library.
14. Ibid.

15. Catherine Clinton, *The Plantation Mistress* (New York: Pantheon Books, 1982), 18.

16. William D. Reeves, *De La Barre: Life of a French Creole Family in Louisiana* (New York: Jefferson Parish Historical Commission, 1980), Monograph IV.

17. Gertrude M. Beauford, "A Tribute to Derbigny," *Jefferson History Notebook*, vol. 2, no. 1, Mar. 1980.

18. Becnel, 41–46.

19. Ibid.

20. Wilson, "Seven Oaks Plantation," HABS.; Reeves with Alario, 24.

21. Reeves with Alario, 25.

22. Becnel, 46.

23. Ibid., 24.

24. Ibid.

Chapter 3

1. Wilson, "Seven Oaks Plantation," HABS.

2. Fred Barry, "Seven Oaks," *New Orleans Times-Picayune*, 29 Feb. 1976.

3. Ibid.

4. Davis Jahncke, professional architect, interview by author, New Orleans, July 2001.

5. Wilson, "Famous La. Plantation Mansion Crumbling to Ruins Across River."

6. Samuel Wilson Jr., *A Guide to Early Architecture of New Orleans* (New Orleans: American Institute of Architects); Pie Dufour, "Preview of Seven Oaks," *New Orleans Times-Picayune*, 5 May 1957; Peter M. Zollman, "Plantation Object of Preservation Drive," *Alexandria Daily Talk Town Talk*, 11 Apr. 1976.

7. Sheryl H. Parker, Seven *Oaks Plantation*, thesis, Special Collections of Tulane University; New Orleans, Louisiana.

8. Ibid.

9. Davis Jahncke, architect, interview by the author, New Orleans, July 2001.

10. Wilson, "Famous La. Plantation Mansion Crumbling to Ruins Across River."

11. John Pope, "When it was home . . ." *States Item*, 6 June 1977, sec. B.; Davis Jahncke, Architectural Drawings, personal collection.

12. Wilson, "Seven Oaks Plantation," HABS.

13. Reeves with Alario, 34–35.

14. Pitts; Pope, "When it was home . . ."

15. Wilson, "Seven Oaks Plantation," HABS; Davis Jahncke, interview with the author; Wilson, "Famous La. Plantation Mansion Crumbling to Ruins Across River."

16. Parker, 2; Wilson, "Seven Oaks Plantation," HABS.

17. Pitts.

18. Reeves with Alario.

19. John B. Rehder, *Delta Sugar: Louisiana's Vanishing Plantation Landscape* (Baltimore: Johns Hopkins University Press, 1999), 70–87.
20. Zimple's 1834 map probably shows the earlier Zeringue house. Regardless, the formal gardens would have been in place at both houses, once construction was complete.
21. Crété, 255–56.
22. Rehder, 61–65.
23. Ibid.
24. Ibid., 103–5.
25. Peter Kolchin, *American Slavery 1619–1877* (New York: Hill and Wang, 1993), 114; 1860 U.S. Census, Jefferson Parish Slave Schedule. See Appendix IV of this volume for comparative data.
26. Crété, 256–57.
27. Charles P. Roland, *Louisiana Sugar Plantations During the American Civil War* (Leiden: E. J. Brill, 1957); Kolchin, 113.
28. Ibid.
29. George P. Rawick, ed., *The American Slave: A Composite Autobiography.* (Westport, Conn.: Greenwood Press, 1979).
30. John Michael Vlach, *Back of the Big House: The Architecture of Plantation Slavery* (Chapel Hill: University of North Carolina Press, 1993).
31. Letter from Sister Aliqout to Father Stephen Rousselon, Mar. 19, 1852. Archdiocesan Archives, Archdioceses of New Orleans.
32. National Archives of the Society of the Sacred Heart. *Lettres Anuelles, 1924–26,* 2:345–51 (the biography of Camille Zeringue), *Lettres Anuelles, 1921–23,* 2:348–49 (the biography of Marie Celeste Zeringue), and *Lettres Anuelles, 1927–29,* 2:340–44 (the biography of Marie Ann Lise Zeringue). It was the custom of the Society of the Sacred Heart to write short biographies of deceased members to be preserved in the Society's records. Stories, anecdotes, descriptions, and a career chronology were often included. These records were compiled in the Lettres Anuelles. Thanks to the late Sharon Favre and Kermit Venable for translation assistance.
33. W. E. Butler, *Down Among The Sugarcane* (Baton Rouge: Moran Publishing Corporation, 1990), 6.
34. Solomon Northup, *Twelve Years A Slave*, ed. Sue Eakin and Joseph Logsdon (Baton Rouge: Louisiana State University Press, 1968), 161–62.

Chapter 4

1. See Appendix III for more information.
2. Crété, 26; Joseph Karl Menn, *The Large Slaveholders of Louisiana, 1860* (New Orleans: Pelican Publishing Company, 1964), 63.
3. Roland, 30.

4. Without question, the grinding season was the most labor-intensive time of the year. As cane was harvested by one gang of slaves, another waited to haul it to the sugarhouse. The production of sugar from cane continued, virtually nonstop, from October to January. An air of excitement ran through the entire plantation as a great effort was made to produce as much sugar as possible while the cane was still fresh. Every slave—man, woman, and child—worked eighteen hours a day in shifts, so that production was continuous. Such intense labor was grueling for the slaves, and masters often enticed them with food, liquor, tobacco, and coffee. The grinding season was a time of paradox.

5. In this context, a hogshead refers to a measurement roughly equal to one barrel or one thousand pounds.

6. P. A. Champomier, *Statement of the Sugar Crop Made in Louisiana in 1849–50* (New Orleans: Cook, Young and Company, 1850); Menn, 257–58.

7. When shipping sugar to New Orleans to be sold, if the market was depressed and the sugar did not fetch a minimum bid, it would be stored in a warehouse until the market was more favorable. This method of marketing sugar was least favored by planters. It meant that they would not know the price the sugar would fetch when it left the plantation and that the sugar could possibly be held for a long time, incurring various fees for the planter, for transportation and storage, and for the factor responsible for marketing the sugar on the levee. Walter Prichard, "Routine on a Louisiana Sugar Plantation under the Slavery Regime," *Mississippi Valley Historical Review* 14, no. 2 (Sept. 1927): 168–78.

8. Cotton, then crowned as "King Cotton," became a booming success after the invention of the cotton gin. By 1834, Alabama, Mississippi, and Louisiana grew more than half the nation's supply of cotton. By 1859, Georgia joined those three states in producing nearly 80 percent of the nation's cotton.

9. The Inflation Calculator, http://www.westegg.com/inflation/infl.cgi

10. *Lettres Annuelles 1924–26*, 2:345–51; *1921–23*, 2:348–49; *1927–29*, 2:340–44, Society of the Sacred Heart National Archives.

11. There was also an older daughter who is not listed in the census of 1850, according to the *Lettres Annuelles*.

12. *Lettres Annuelles, 1924–26*, 2:345–51; *1921–23*, 2:348–49; *1927–29*, 2:340–44, Society of the Sacred Heart National Archives.

13. Roland, 13.

14. *Lettres Annuelles, 1924–26*, 2:345–51; *1921–23*, 2:348–49; *1927–29*, 2:340–44, Society of the Sacred Heart National Archives.

15. Roland, 13.

16. James Williams, *James Williams, an American Slave, Who Was for Several Years a Driver on a Cotton Plantation in Alabama* (New York: The American Anti-Slavery Society, 1838).

17. Crété, 258–59.
18. Kolchin, 60.
19. From Jefferson Parish Civil Judicial Records. *Jonas Pickles vs. Camille Zeringue.*
    1856. #4053.
20. Ibid.
21. Ibid.
22. Ibid.
23. Ibid.
24. Ibid.
25. Although their name was German, the Zeringues spoke French and adopted
    much of the predominant French culture of the Louisiana planter elite.
26. Crété, 96–97.
27. Ibid., 96.
28. Ibid., 97.
29. A discrepancy of one slave exists between these values and those presented
    earlier from the census. This is likely due to the birth, death, sale, or
    purchase of one slave.
30. For additional information on the Millaudon plantation, see Marc R.
    Matrana, "On Cane and Coolies: Chinese Laborers on Post-Antebellum
    Louisiana Sugar Plantations As Exemplified on the Millaudon Plantation of
    Jefferson Parish," *Jefferson History Notebook* vol. 7, no. 1 (Feb. 2003).
31. The raw data were collected from federal census records and *The Large
    Slaveholders of Louisiana—1860* by Joseph Karl Menn. Statistical data were
    computed by Marc R. Matrana. Numbers were rounded where appropriate.
    See Appendix III for further information.
32. Widow Zeringue, handwritten permission slip to allow a slave baptism.
    Letters and records from Archdiocesan Archives, New Orleans, Louisiana.
33. *Lettres Annuelles, 1924–26,* 2:345–51; *1921–23,* 2:348–49; *1927–29,* 2:340–44,
    Society of the Sacred Heart National Archives.
34. Letter to Father Stephen Rousselon from Sister Marie Aliquot. Letters and
    Records from Archdiocesan Archives, New Orleans, Louisiana.

Chapter 5

1. Roland, 24–25.
2. Eliza Frances Andrews, *The War-Time Journal of a Georgia Girl, 1864–1865*
   (New York: D. Appleton and Company, 1908).
3. Roland, 31.
4. Foreman, vii; Andrew B. Booth, The Booth Papers, *Records of Louisiana
   Confederate Solders and Louisiana Confederate Commands*, p. 1190, originally
   published in New Orleans, 1920, Louisiana State Archives.

5. Arthur W. Bergeron Jr., *Guide to Louisiana Confederate Military Units, 1861–1865* (Baton Rouge: Louisiana State University Press, 1989), 141–42; Stewart Sifakis, *Compendium of the Confederate Armies—Louisiana* (New York: Facts on File, 1995).

6. Roland, 58.

7. *New Orleans Daily Picayune*, Nov. 12, 1861.

8. Mildred Stehle Harris, lecture presentation, Jefferson Historical Society of Louisiana Quarterly Meeting. 8 Dec. 1999.

9. Roland, 129, 131, 135.

10. Ibid., 60.

11. *Lettres Annuelles, 1924–26*, 2:345–51; *1921–23*, 2:348–49; *1927–29*, 2:340–44, Society of the Sacred Heart National Archives.

12. Roland, 56.

13. Lawrence E. Estaville Jr. *Confederate Neckties: Louisiana Railroads in the Civil War* (Ruston, La.: McGinty Publications, 1989).

14. Walter Prichard, "The Effects of the Civil War on the Louisiana Sugar Industry," *Journal of Southern History* 5, no. 3 (Aug. 1939): 315–32.

15. Ibid.

16. "Did you Know?" *Transt Riders' Digest*, 10 May 1976.

17. Roland, 67.

18. *Lettres Annuelles, 1924–26*, 2:345–51; *1921–23*, 2:348–49; *1927–29*, 2:340–44, Society of the Sacred Heart National Archives.

19. Special thanks to the late Sharon Favre of Westwego, Louisiana, a great friend and champion of historic preservation in Westwego and beyond, who spent many hours translating *Lettres Anuelles, 1924–26*, 2:345–51 (the biography of Camille Zeringue) and *Lettres Anuelles, 1921–23*, 2:348–49 (the biography of Marie Celeste Zeringue), and special thanks to Kermit Venable of Gretna, Louisiana, who spent much time translating *Lettres Anuelles, 1927–29*, 2:340–44 (the biography of Marie Ann Lise Zeringue).

20. *Lettres Anuelles, 1924–26*, 2:345–51; *Lettres Anuelles, 1921–23*, 2:348–49; *Lettres Anuelles, 1927–29*, 2:340–44, from the Society of the Sacred Heart National Archives. Information on the sisters' religious lives throughout the rest of this chapter is from these sources.

Chapter 6

1. Prichard, "The Effects of the Civil War on the Louisiana Sugar Industry," 322.

2. George Willard Reed Bayley (c. 1821–1876), known as G. W. R. Bayley, had a colorful career as an engineer in the railroad industry, a historian of railroads in Louisiana, and a state legislator who served as chairman of the House of Representatives Committee on Railroads. His career is meticulously

documented in Walter Prichard's "A Forgotten Louisiana Engineer: G. W. R. Bayley and His 'History of the Railroads of Louisiana,'" *Louisiana Historical Quarterly* 30 (Oct. 1947): 1065–1325.

3. Reeves with Alario.

4. Ibid, 27–28; *New Orleans, Mobile, and Chattanooga vs. Camille Zeringue*, July 1870, Jefferson Parish Judicial (Old) Records.

5. Ibid.

6. Ibid.

7. Ibid.

8. Ibid.

9. "Died Zerinque" (sic) Obituary, *Daily Picayune*. 7 Jan. 1872; Reeves with Alario, 45–48; Edwin Ney Bruce, "Westwego, Louisiana: A Community Study," master's thesis, Thesis Collection, vol. 2, 1947, Tulane University Archives.

10. Reeves with Alario, 32–33.

11. Ibid.

12. Swanson, *Historic Jefferson Parish, From Shore to Shore*, 85; Corley; Pitts; Wilson, "Famous La. Plantation Mansion Crumbling to Ruins Across River."

13. Wilson, "Seven Oaks," HABS; Reeves with Alario.

14. "Madeline Lisa (sic) Roman Zeringue" Obituary, *New Orleans Daily Picayune*, 17 Apr. 1892.

Chapter 7

1. "Did You Know?"

2. Reeves with Alario, 35–36; "Did you Know?"; Advertisement, *New Orleans Daily Picayune*, 7 July 1893.

3. Swanson, *Historic Jefferson Parish: From Shore to Shore*, 85.

4. Advertisement, *New Orleans Daily Picayune*, July 1893.; Reeves with Alario, 35–36.

5. Advertisement, *New Orleans Daily Picayune*, 24 May 1893.

6. "Columbia Gardens," *New Orleans Daily Picayune*, 24 May 1893; Advertisement, *New Orleans Daily Picayune*, July 1893.

7. Reeves with Alario, 48, 168–69; Rehder, 152–256.

8. Ibid.

9. Bruce.

10. Reeves with Alario, 56.

11. Wilson, "Seven Oaks Plantation," HABS.

12. Lloyd F. Giardina, Jefferson Parish Councilman, interview by the author, 21 June 2001; Anthony Giardina, interview by the author, July 2001.

13. Ibid.

14. Ibid.

15. Reeves with Alario, 36; "Another deadline for Seven Oaks," *New Orleans States-Item*, 10 May 1977.

Chapter 8

1. Fred Barry, "Seven Oaks," *New Orleans Times-Picayune*, 29 Feb. 1976; Barry, "Once Splendid Orleans Mansion Now Crumbling Towards Death"; Corley.

2. Mildred Stehle Harris, interview by author, Sept. 2000.

3. Memo from Major E. L. Higdon, the Commanding Officer of the 4th Battalion of the United States Guards, Headquarters, 4th Battalion United States Guards, Camp Beauregard, Louisiana, to the Adjunct General of the Army, Washington, D.C., 26 Dec. 1918.

4. Mildred Stehle Harris, interview by the author, Sept. 2000.

5. John Pope, "History is bulldozed at Seven Oaks," *New Orleans States-Item*, 5 Sept. 1977.

6. Mildred Stehle Harris, interview by the author, Sept. 2000.

7. Andrea Taylor, Doris Taylor Pichoff, and Dr. Bruce Pichoff, series of interviews by the author, 2000–01.

8. Ibid.

9. Ibid.

10. Reeves with Alario, 35–36.; Loretta P. Brehm, interview by the author, 2001.

11. Reeves with Alario, 36–41; Mildred Stehle Harris, interview by the author.

12. John Pope, "When it was home . . ." *New Orleans States-Item*, 6 June 1977, sec. B.

13. Mildred Stehle Harris, lecture presentation, Jefferson Historical Society of Louisiana Quarterly Meeting, 8 Dec. 1999; Mildred Stehle Harris, interview by the author.

14. Pope, "When it was home . . ."; Reeves with Alario, 36–37; Harris, interview with the author.

15. Reeves with Alario, 37; Mildred Stehle Harris, interview with the author.

16. Ibid.

17. Pope, "When it was home . . .".

18. Mildred Stehle Harris, interview with the author.

19. Reeves with Alario.

20. Mildred Stehle Harris, interview with the author; Reeves and Alario, 39; Pope, "When it was home . . .".

21. Mildred Stehle Harris, interview with the author; Barry, "Once Splendid Orleans Mansion Crumbling Towards Death."

22. Reeves with Alario, 39. In October 2001, Louisiana State Archeologist Robb Mann visited the site of Seven Oaks plantation along with the author of this volume and Westwego Historical Society president and author Daniel P. Alario Sr. Mann was extremely impressed with the potential for archeological study of the site considering its significant past (especially as an early slave depot) and because of its relatively untouched condition. He has advocated that such an endeavor be undertaken. It is the hope of the community that such a project will materialize and that the current property owners will cooperate with these important efforts.

23. Mildred Stehle Harris, lecture presentation, Jefferson Historical Society of Louisiana Quarterly Meeting, 8 Dec. 1999.

24. Pope, "When it was home . . ."; Reeves with Alario, 39–40; Mildred Stehle Harris, interview with the author.

25. Ibid.

26. Ibid.

27. Reeves with Alario, 35–40.

28. Pope, "When it was home . . ."; Mildred Stehle Harris, interview with the author.

29. John Pope, "History is Bulldozed at Seven Oaks," *New Orleans States-Item*, 5 Sept. 1977; Mildred Stehle Harris, interview with the author.

Chapter 9

1. Corely; "Seven Oaks," *Préservation*, Louisiana Landmarks Society, Mar. 1957; Pie Dufour, "Preview of Seven Oaks," *New Orleans Times-Picayune*, 5 May 1957; Barry, "Once Splendid Orleans Mansion Now Crumbling Towards Death."

2. Ibid.; "Seven Oaks Plantation, Westwego: The Roof's On—What Next?" *Préservation*, Louisiana Landmarks Society, Aug. 1957.

3. "Trespassing Permitted . . . Today Only," *Dixie Roto, New Orleans Times-Picayune*, 11 May 1958.

4. "Seven Oaks," *Préservation*, Louisiana Landmarks Society, July 1958; Barry, "Once Splendid Orleans Mansion Now Crumbling Towards Death."

5. Barry, "Once Splendid Orleans Mansion Now Crumbling Towards Death"; Pitts; Corley; Zollman.

6. Herschel Miller, "Goodbye Seven Oaks," *New Orleans*, May 1969: 28–31.

7. "State Landmark Group Sets N.O. Meet Tomorrow," *State Times*, 27 May 1969.

8. Ibid.; Barry, "Once Splendid Orleans Mansion Now Crumbling Towards Death."

9. Ibid.

10. Miller.

11. Keith Kaiser, "Effort Will Be Made to Restore Ancient Mansion," *West Bank Guide*, 21 June 1967; Barry, "Once Splendid Orleans Mansion Now Crumbling Towards Death."

12. John Pope, "Don Lee Keith, 62, writer, instructor," Obituary, *New Orleans Times-Picayune*, 30 July 2003.

13. John McMillan, "Capote vs. Seven Oaks," *Dixie Roto Magizine, New Orleans Times-Picayune*, 17 June 1973, p. 10+.

14. Ibid.

Chapter 10

1. Corley.

2. Ibid.

3. Fred Barry, "Fate of Seven Oaks," *New Orleans Times-Picayune*, 14 Mar. 1976

4. Ibid.; Corley.

5. Corley.

6. Barry, "Fate of Seven Oaks"; John Pope, "A forward step for Jeff history?" *States-Item*, 19 Jan. 1977.

7. Fred Barry, "Bid to Save Mansion Accelerates," *New Orleans Times-Picayune*, 20 Mar. 1976.

8. Ibid.

9. "Jeff Plans to Preserve Seven Oaks," *New Orleans Times-Picayune*, 26 Mar. 1976.

10. "Save 7 Oaks Call Heeded," *New Orleans Times-Picayune*, 8 Apr. 1976.

11. Fred Barry, "7 Oaks Grant Request Okayed by Jeff Council," *New Orleans Times-Picayune*, 9 Apr. 1976; Fred Barry, "State Funds Available to Restore Seven Oaks," *New Orleans Times-Picayune*, 6 Apr. 1976.

12. "Wego Board Agrees to Back Restoration," *New Orleans Times-Picayune*, 13 Apr. 1976.

13. "Jeff Council Hit by Alario," *New Orleans Times-Picayune*, 13 Apr. 1976.

14. "Plea for Seven Oaks Goes to Panel," *New Orleans Times-Picayune*, 27 July 1976.

15. "Another deadline for Seven Oaks," *New Orleans States-Item*, 10 May 1977.

16. "Jesse James Deleted in Mansion Resolution," *New Orleans Times-Picayune*, 21 Aug. 1976.

17. "Seven Oaks Is Denied Federal Aid," *New Orleans Times-Picayune*, 2 Sept. 1976.

18. "Jeff Council Turns Back on Seven Oaks Home," *New Orleans Times-Picayune*, 10 Sept. 1976.

19. Lloyd Giardina, Jefferson Parish Councilman, interview by the author, 21 June 2001.

20. Pope, "Stay of execution may save 7 Oaks."
21. Fred Barry, "Demolition of Ruins Extended 6 Months," *New Orleans Times-Picayune*, 9 Nov. 1976; Pope, "Stay of execution may save 7 oaks."
22. Ibid.
23. Pope, "Seven Oaks wins stay of execution."
24. Joan Treadway, "Plantation Must Go—Unless," *New Orleans Times-Picayune*, 10 May 1977.
25. "Another Deadline for Seven Oaks," *New Orleans States-Item*, 10 May 1977.
26. Betsy Swanson, interview by the author, 17 Aug. 2001.
27. Corley; John Pope, "History is bulldozed at Seven Oaks," *New Orleans States-Item*, 5 Sept. 1977.
28. Corley; Tom Frazer, "Seven Oaks Plantation torn down, carted off," *New Orleans States-Item*, 30 Aug. 1977.
29. Corley.
30. Ibid.; Pope, "History is bulldozed at Seven Oaks."

Chapter 11

1. All information in this chapter came from Kay Andressen, interview by the author, Kenner, La., 31 July 1999.
2. Traditionally in southeastern Louisiana, large barges made their way down the Mississippi River with goods but were unable to make the return visit upriver due to the strong currents. These barges were disassembled and the wood was often used for construction of various houses and buildings.

Chapter 12

1. Marc R. Matrana, "Old mansion gone forever," letter to the editor, *New Orleans Times-Picayune*, 9 Aug. 2003, B-6; Robert Hosch Jr., "Plantation restoration is key," letter to the editor, *New Orleans Times-Picayune*, 2 Aug. 2003, B-6.
2. Jennifer L. Eichstedt and Stephen Small, *Representations of Slavery, Race and Ideology in Southern Plantation Museums* (Washington, D.C.: Smithsonian Institution Press, 2002).
3. Chizuko Izawa, "A Captivating Tale and the Urgency of Reconstructing Seven Oaks," unpublished report, 2001.

Appendix I

1. William D. Reeves with Daniel Alario Sr., *Westwego, From Cheniere to Canal* (Westwego, La.: Published privately by Mr. and Mrs. Daniel Alario Sr., 1996), 22.

2. Samuel Wilson Jr., "Seven Oaks Plantation," HABS.

3. "Did you Know?" *Transt Riders' Digest*, 10 May 1976; Betsy Swanson and Bethlyn McCloskey, "The Saga of Seven Oaks," *Preservation Press*, vol 3, no. 1, Oct. 1976.

Appendix IV

1. John Hanno Deiler, *The Settlement of the German Coast of Louisiana and The Creoles of German Descent*, updated by Jack Belson (Baltimore: Genealogical Publishing Company, 1969); Agnes Rita Zeringue Foreman, *Zerangue, Zeringue, Zyrangue and Allied Families* (Baltimore: Gateway Press, Inc., 1979).

2. Albert J. Robichaux Jr., *German Coast Families, European Origins and Settlement in Colonial Louisiana* (Rayne, La.: Hebert Publications, 1997), 378.

3. Ibid., 379.

4. Ibid., 380; Foreman, 1.

5. Foreman, iv; Deiler; Marcel Giraud, *A History of French Louisiana, Vol. 5, The Company of the Indies, 1723–1731*, trans. Brian Pearce (Baton Rouge: Louisiana State University Press, 1991), 232–33.; Robichaux, 382.

6. Robichaux, 382.

7. Ibid.

8. Samuel Wilson Jr., *Bienville's New Orleans, A French Colonial Capital, 1718–1768* (New Orleans: The Friends of the Cabildo); Wall, 85; Leonard V. Huber and Samuel Wilson Jr., *The Basilica on Jackson Square* (New Orleans: Saint Louis Cathedral, 1965), 6.

9. Robichaux, 382; Roger Baudier, *The Catholic Church in Louisiana* (New Orleans, 1939; reprint, Louisiana Library Association, Public Library Section, 1972), 81.

10. Huber and Wilson.

11. Foreman, iv.

12. Ibid.

13. For the sake of clarity and to eliminate confusion between Michael Zerhinger/ Zeringue/Seringue/Sering and his grandson, Michael Zeringue who owned Petit Desert, when referring to the elder Michael, this volume uses the earlier spelling of his name, "Zerhinger," as he himself signed it on the passenger list of the ship *Le Domadaire*, which carried him and his family to Louisiana from France. "Michael Zeringue" refers to the younger Michael, grandson of the carpenter.

14. Huber and Wilson.

15. Ibid., 6–7.

16. Robichaux, 383; *Louisiana Purchase*, exhibition guide (New Orleans: Louisiana State Museum and The Louisiana Landmarks Society, 1953), 15.

17. Baudier, 107.
18. Ibid.
19. *Louisiana Purchase*, 17
20. Huber and Wilson, 9–10.
21. Ibid.
22. *Johann Michael Zeringue*. Zeringue On-Line. www.desertsky.net/zol/ johannmichael.html
23. Robichaux, 383.
24. Foreman.
25. Huber and Wilson.
26. Stanley Clisby Arthur, *Old New Orleans* (Gretna, La.: Pelican Publishing Company, 1990).

INDEX

Housing and Urban Development,
U.S. Department of. *See* HUD
Houze, Luther, 108
Huber, Leonard, 100–1
HUD, 114, 117
Huey P. Long Bridge, 92, 107, 134, 135
Hughes, David, 108

Iberville, Pierre Le Moyne, sieur d', 3
Innovative Projects Program in
Neighborhood Preservation, 117
Isle of Orleans. *See* New Orleans
Izawa, Chizuko, 135

Jahncke, Davis, 134
Jefferson, Thomas, 15, 20
Jefferson Historical Society of
Louisiana, 96
Jefferson Parish, 20–21, 22, 45–46,
104–7, 112; Advisory Board on
Environmental Development,
105–6; Historical Commission, 112,
131; Police Jury, 21, 60, 98
Jefferson Rangers, 60
Jefferson Station, 62, 65
Jesse James Memorial Site, 116
Jesse K. Belle, 82
Johnson, Henry, 20
Jonchere, Gerard Michel de la, 4
Juan Luis (a slave), 13

Keith, Don Lee, 108–9
Kenner, 126
Kinder-Morgan, 131

LaBranche, L., 24
Lafayette, 20
LaFourche, Bayou, 25–26
LaFourche Levee Board, 97
Laroussini Street, 86

La Salle, Rene Robert Cavelier,
sieur de, 3
Laura Plantation, 134
Law, John, 4
Lawson, James E., Jr., 117
Lazy River Landing, 134
Lebeau House, 131
LeBlanc, Monseigner, 4, 8
Lebreton, L. C., 76
Lebreton, Noël B., 13, 24
Lelong, Alphonse A., 86
Levy, Jules, 81, 84
Limberg-An-Der-Lahn, Germany, 30
Lincoln, Abraham, 65
Little True Vine, 67. *See also* True Vine
Livaudais, Francois Enoul, 25
L'Orient, Port of, 4
Louisiana Act, 24, 38
Louisiana Department of Art, History,
and Cultural Preservation, 117
Louisiana Landmark Society, 100–2, 107
Louisiana Purchase, 16, 20
Louisiana Street, 86
Louis XIV (king of France), 3

Mabel Comeaux, 82
Mace, A., 19
Maison, Joseph, 10
Marcello, Joseph, 119
Marrero, Louis H., Sr., 87
Martin, Theodore H., 89
Massey, Jean Baptiste, 9
Matrana, Frank, Jr., 95
Matrana, Frank, Sr., 95
Matrana, Nicolo, 95
May, George, 53–54
McCloskey, Bethlyn, 105, 119–21
McDonogh, John, 14
McGhee, Thomas L., 53
Merriam, E. G., 86
Metzler, Mother, 69
Mexico, Gulf of, 61

Printed in the United States
42428LVS00006B/28-147

9 781578 069002